Plato's Po

Mark Vernon is a writer, journalist, academic, and former priest. Author of several books, including *42 : Deep Thought on Life, the Universe, and Everything*, he is an Honorary Research Fellow at Birkbeck College, University of London, and a regular contributor to BBC radio and television. He is on the faculty of The School of Life in London.

Plato's Podcasts

The Ancients' Guide to Modern Living

Mark Vernon

ONEWORLD
OXFORD

A Oneworld Paperback Original

Published by Oneworld Publications 2009

Copyright © Mark Vernon 2009

The right of Mark Vernon to be identified as the
Author of this work has been asserted by him in accordance with the
Copyright, Designs and Patents Act 1988

ISBN 978–1–85168–706–0

Typeset by Jayvee, Trivandrum, India
Cover design by Patrick Knowles
Printed and bound in Great Britain by
the CPI Group

Oneworld Publications
UK: 185 Banbury Road, Oxford, OX2 7AR, England
USA: 38 Greene Street, 4th Floor, New York, NY 10013, USA
www.oneworld-publications.com

In memory of Paul Fletcher who brought philosophy to life along with pretty much everything else.

Contents

Acknowledgements

It is too anachronistic to thank the authors of antiquity upon whom I draw, the eminent, forgotten and curious philosophers themselves, as well as those who 'recorded' their words, notably Diogenes Laertius. However, a number of contemporary scholars of antiquity have proven invaluable too.

I would particularly recommend the scholarly and accessible series 'Ancient Philosophies' published by Acumen. It is superb and fills a gaping hole in the market. John Sellars' *Stoicism*, William Desmond's *Cynics*, James Warren's *Presocratics* and Pauliina Remes' *Neoplatonism* have been at my side whilst writing. The indispensable volume for framing the approach I've taken – looking at life as well as thought, seeing ancient philosophy as a practice – is laid out by Pierre Hadot in *What Is Ancient Philosophy?* (Belknap Press), again a clear and penetrating read. Trevor Curnow's *The Philosophers of the Ancient World: An A–Z Guide* (Duckworth) is a handy and exhaustive reference: he lists over 2,300 of them. He has also written a short essay, *Ancient Philosophy and Everyday Life* (Cambridge Scholars Press) that set me thinking. Some useful, short essays can be found in *Meet the Philosophers of Ancient Greece: everything you always wanted to know about ancient Greek philosophy but didn't know how to ask*, edited by Patricia F. O'Grady (Ashgate): it is not as frivolous as it sounds. All the translations of ancient Greek and Roman texts are from standard sources. In particular, Diogenes Laertius is taken from R.D. Hicks' version of *Lives of Eminent Philosophers* in the Loeb Classical Library. The other translation particularly to note is that of Sappho's poetry fragments, which are by the poet and classicist Anne Carson.

At Oneworld I would like to thank Mike Harpley very much for commissioning the book; John Sellars, Mike again and an anonymous reader for performing the non-trivial task of commenting on an earlier version of the manuscript. And I recall that the idea stemmed in part from a conversation with Dan Bunyard: thanks again to him too.

Illustrations

Introduction

There are periods in history when it feels as if almost everything is changing. The economic prosperity that one generation enjoyed is thrown into doubt for the next. There are dramatic shifts in the balance of power, as new political forces appear on the horizon, causing the old consensus to flounder. The daily lives of ordinary people are transformed by sudden progress in the sciences, and are astonishing and unsettling in equal measure. Such moments are commonly regarded warily. They precipitate moral panics, ideological fundamentalism and suspicion amongst neighbours.

They are also times in which some individuals are inspired to dig deep. These rare souls turn again to questions about what it is to be human, what it is to flourish, and out of their enquiries emerge profound insights. They sometimes forge a new philosophy of life that can sustain their fellows for centuries.

Much was up for grabs in the time of Plato and his peers. It is no coincidence that philosophy, the love of wisdom, was born during this turbulent period of history – in which one war or another was usually being waged, and in which democracy was established and then fell. The first philosophers who inquired into the nature of things, questioned the gods and encouraged others to think about how they lived, were a rag-bag of individuals. They knew they were onto something substantial. But they would never have guessed that, first, their ideas would evolve into traditions of thought and practice that others would follow for a millennium. And then, after the arrival of Christianity, that we would still know them by name and ponder their perceptions to this day.

There is good reason to think that we are living through another era of change. The collapse of the banking system in 2008 will certainly go down as seismic in economic history. By causing uncertainty and challenging consumerism, it has encouraged millions to rethink their lives. And that must be seen in a broader context: the shift in the balance of power from the West to the East; the emergence of a plural society in which every day you might encounter people whose beliefs are different from your own; and the potentially devastating impact of climate change. Now, it can be argued, is a good time to think about what it's all about. One way of doing so is to return to roots. So just what was ancient philosophy?

Well, here's one thing to note: Plato wrote dialogues. They portray real characters engaged in the messy business of working out what they believed in life. When you think about it, that was an astonishing thing to do. You'd think a philosopher would want to devise watertight proofs, like an Isaac Newton, not write literature, like a Shakespeare who artfully hides himself in his plays. Nothing could be further from what is called philosophy today. But, so far as we know, Plato did not write a single monograph, treatise or book.

The reason is that a good dialogue invites readers to reconsider what they themselves think. Moreover, it draws them in, so they don't just have to weigh their reasons but their feelings, convictions, character and habits too. Then comes the challenge: are you going to change? For like a play or a novel, a dialogue is not just about the rational content of people's heads, it can encompass how they live, body and soul. To read a dialogue is, therefore, to be encouraged to muse on how you live too. A dialogue might be said to be like a guide – a book of possibilities that presents the choices you might make, and worries over how you might come to terms with them.

Plato's dialogues were hugely successful. Writing had been around for some centuries before he, or his secretary, put quill to papyrus in the 390s BCE. But it was only relatively recently that memorised poems had given way to written texts as the preferred means of communicating ideas. The dialogue exploited a new technology. They were read by individuals, and then copied and commended to friends. Like podcasts on the internet today, they spread out like virtual ripples of thought across the ancient Mediterranean world. They left people wanting more. They were provocations to do philosophy, to chew over the innovative, 'modern' ways of life they conveyed.

As we explore what these ancient Greeks and Romans might have to say about life today, we will consider more than just Plato's 'podcasts'. We will meet many other key characters along the way: the book is not itself a dialogue but it is a kind of conversation amongst them – and often an argument, for they disagreed about the good life.

They claimed as their own a freedom of speech – *parrhesia* in Greek, the right to say what's on your mind in an effort to pierce the clouds of delusion and arrive at truth. This was a rare art in antiquity. Ancient politics taught men to speak evasively, if not with outright guile. Candour could get you killed. A citizen could expect frankness from only two individuals, his wife and – if he was lucky enough to know one – a philosopher, his

Figure 1 Bust of Plato, Roman copy of Greek original

guru, you might say. Some of what these philosophers uttered was slightly mad. Some of it changed the course of history. They also lived together, in community. They practised a way of life, the practice and the free-thought being inseparable for them. Merely to talk about philosophy would be like buying a cookery book and never turning on the stove. If the proof of the pudding is in the eating, the proof of philosophy was in the living.

The philosophers used to say that thought is therapy, and over the centuries they devised a range of different therapies, coupled to different schools of thought – Peripatetics, Stoics, Cynics, Epicureans and others. From about the fifth century BCE, a citizen of Athens had the luxury of choice as he or she searched for a guru at whose feet to sit, and from whom to work out his or her own philosophy of life. Some were extreme, demanding that you own next-to-nothing, roll in hot sand, live in a barrel and/or make love in public. Others were just difficult, demanding a complete reorientation of your view of things. Philosophy can be tough. But if it is difficult solely because it has become technical or abstract, as academic philosophy is at risk of becoming today, then it has probably lost sight of its primary goal.

To put it another way, the greatest philosophers were not just people who could argue well. They were that rare individual who not only thinks and sees clearly, but is, as a result, actually good. Socrates was such an individual for many ancient Greeks. That is why he is not just a great intellectual figure but an axial figure, to use Karl Jaspers' term: his significance is comparable to that of Jesus or the Buddha. He was a prophet, someone whose life challenged his times, and ours.

He attracted his critics too, of course, and there were some who preferred to think of him solely in relation to his admittedly odd characteristics: he wore no shoes, drank until dawn though without getting drunk, refused even the most beautiful

Figure 2 Socrates, from a wall painting in an ancient Roman house

of Athenian men, and, perhaps unsurprisingly, was loathed by his wife. But the point is that he was known as much for his life as his thought.

The stories of the ancient philosophers' exploits, habits, encounters and conversations were staples of antiquity and the Middle Ages. There was Diogenes who told Alexander where to get off; Secundus who took a vow of silence apparently as a result of an unspeakable encounter with his mother; and Hipparchia who could have married anyone but chose a man who looked like a twig and lived like one too. Others suffered for their sagacity working like slaves, fleeing tyrants whom they'd offended, and dying all manner of unpleasant deaths. These weren't just amusing anecdotes, though some of them are that. They were more than mythical stories, though the tales that come down to us often idealise the philosopher concerned. The narratives of their lives conveyed what they were about quite as clearly as the words they uttered during their lives.

This was understood by one writer who has become very important now, Diogenes Laertius. He lived in the third century CE. When he decided to compile a record of ancient philosophy, it seemed quite natural to him to gather the stories, to turn to the lives of these sages. It is clear that some of what Laertius pasted together in his *Lives of Eminent Philosophers* is questionable. It can be apocryphal, though entertaining and transmitting grains of truth. And much of the material is straightforwardly illuminating. Michel de Montaigne, the sixteenth-century essayist who has been called the French Socrates, put it well:

I am deeply sorry that we do not have Diogenes Laertiuses by the dozen, or that he himself did not spread himself more widely or more wisely, for I consider the lives and fortunes of the great teachers of mankind no less carefully than their ideas and doctrines.

In this book, we will look at the lives and fortunes of some of the most important, some of the frequently forgotten and some of the most eccentric of these ancient teachers. The aim is to reflect on them and so reflect on our own lives. We will ask what they have to say to us as we grapple with what we count as important, and build a way of life that tries to pursue it.

Of course, it might be thought entertaining but anachronistic to look to the ancients for advice on living now. Were not their problems vastly different from ours? Are not their solutions dated, untenable or possibly distasteful by contemporary standards? Well, ask yourself who wrote this: 'Today most people favour the life of consumption and pursue pleasure or wealth or fame.' It was Aristotle, 2,500 years ago. Or how about this:

> The Rulers, who are in power because they have amassed so much wealth, do not want to prohibit by law the extravagance of the young, and stop them from wasting their money and ruining themselves. Their intention is to make loans to such imprudent people or by buying up their property to hope to increase their own wealth and influence ... The moneymakers continue to inject the toxic sting of their loans wherever they can.

It was Plato, and it sounds remarkably familiar. There are revolutions in this world and history can separate people and places by great distances. But enough remains constant, particularly perhaps in the realm of life's great truths, for us to make good sense of them.

In fact, the distance of the ancient schools is a positive asset because the unfamiliar setting can render their perennial insights remarkably fresh. There is the Epicurean thought that most of the desires that trouble us are not desires for things that are necessary but for things we only think we need. Or the Sceptics' insight that much of our anxiety comes from trying to decide about matters on which we can never hope to reach a settled mind. We will consider the Cynics' conviction that life goes wrong when it moves too far from what is natural. And the Stoic observation that life goes well when we live as part of the cosmic whole.

Ancient philosophy can be striking for another reason. It is inspiring – inspiring because its founding figures were deeply impressive characters. Pyrrho managed to practise a genuine indifference to the tittle-tattle of city life. Epicurus provoked something close to a personality cult because of his humility and courage. Socrates was loved not so much for what he said (and he wrote nothing) but because he struck people as being saintly. That spirit still speaks across the centuries. As emperor Julian, the last pagan head of the Empire, observed: the schools were 'in some ways a universal philosophy'. Very many ordinary people – not just men, but women and slaves – dedicated themselves to such matters. Philosophy was about what you ate, how you had sex, where you lived. Get those choices right and think less squiffily too, and it promised the good life.

Out of this treasure-trove, we will start with two figures who lived before Socrates, and end with the great man himself, though otherwise our exploration proceeds in roughly historical order. The biographies, in their historical reality and mythical accretions, lead to insights which we will unpack too. They are ancient lives but they perhaps still speak to modern living.

CHAPTER 1

Pythagoras and the search for meaning

Human beings are meaning-seeking creatures. We attach value to people, things and places like a shopkeeper who knows the price of every product in the shop. Significance is central to living. Without it the human animal dies. We cannot tell whether a whale finds the song of its fellows beautiful, or if the bee perceives the exquisite nature of the flower as it buzzes in. We immediately sense both. It's part and parcel of our being in the world. Meaning is basic. Without it, there would be little point in proceeding any further with our guide.

And yet, much in modern life calls that search for meaning into question, even mocks it. Are we just the playthings of selfish genes? Is love no more than a rush of hormones to the head? Are the patterns and order we detect in the cosmos just illusions, a purposefulness that we read into nature that is not objectively there? That they may be a trick of appearance is sometimes referred to as the disenchantment of the world. Nietzsche spotted this loss of value when, at the turn of the twentieth century, he declared the death of God. He did not literally mean that a divinity had died, for he did not believe that any divinity previously existed. Rather, he said, we have 'unchained this earth from its sun'; we are now 'straying as through an infinite nothing'; life feels as if it has become 'colder'.

Something of the same melancholia was in the air at the birth of ancient philosophy. The sophist Protagoras summed it up when he declared that he could not be sure the gods exist and so man himself must be the 'measure of things', if things were still to be thought valuable. Alternatively the playwright Euripides puts the following prayer into the mouth of Hecuba, in *The Women of Troy*: 'Zeus, whoever thou art, upholding the earth, throned above the earth, whether human intelligence or natural law, mysterious and unknown …'. Replace 'Zeus' with 'God' and that could be the prayer of a modern agnostic.

Others, such as Plato, objected. Life has meaning because life is indeed meaningful, they insisted. The very fact of our existence in the world is amazing, or at least it is for most people. But can that be shown or proven? For that, Plato and others turned to someone who had lived before them all. This individual and his followers had argued that science itself is a meaning-revealing exercise. In fact, the purer the science, the more potent its insights – which is why they loved maths. The individual was called Pythagoras.

Of all the strange things that are remembered about ancient philosophers, none are weirder than those associated with Pythagoras. He is a man of mystery, indeed a man of pure myth, some scholars have said – but then scholars are in the doubting business. For example, his inner thigh was said to be made of gold. Rivers were heard speaking to him. He reportedly had a photographic memory, and could recall the details of everything that had ever happened to him in this life – and in past lives too, for he believed in the transmigration of souls. This retention was a gift from the god Hermes.

Talking of retention, he was remarkably anal about food. Red mullet was a particular loathing, along with eggs. He advised that one should only have sex in winter, and never in summer. And yet, if you wanted to follow him, such abstinence would have been the least of your worries. First, potential disciples had to keep silent for five years. Then, they had to listen to his discourses without actually seeing him: like a bat, he only came out at night.

Travelling to the Ionian island of Samos today, the birthplace of Pythagoras, you would not think to doubt his historical existence. The main town is called Pythagorio. Greeting visitors on the jetty is an inspiring, geometric statue of the (presumably) sixth-century BCE philosopher, mathematician and musician. It reflects the theorem to which the name of Pythagoras is given, the sage's hand reaching to the top corner of a triangle, thereby

Figure 3 Pythagoras as a symbol for Arithmetic, from Palazzo Ducale in Venice (Photo: Giovanni Dall'Orto)

completing the three sides. On the coppery base are quotations celebrating the harmony of the universe, also known as the music of the spheres.

Once one of the wealthiest islands in the Aegean Sea, and close to the Asia Minor mainland that is modern day Turkey, the story goes that the youthful Pythagoras travelled around the Mediterranean – 'journeying amongst the Chaldeans and Magi,' as Diogenes Laertius puts it – and found his way to Egypt, land of the sun god Ra. Here he discovered a mix of mysticism and geometry, as supremely symbolised in the Great Pyramids of Giza. It was to fascinate him for the rest of his life. He came to believe that orbs and circles are the most beautiful objects, and that the earth and heavens must be spherical too, not cylindrical or flat as was also proposed at the time. He came to believe that even numbers can be thought of as female, rounded, warm; and that odd numbers are male, angular, anomalous. It sounds mad until you notice that odd numbers are indeed often quite 'odd', as in 'peculiar'. For example, all the prime numbers, bar 2, are odd, and prime numbers – those numbers that are only divisible by themselves and the unity one – are peculiar indeed.

At some point, he returned to Samos, only to flee to Croton in Italy when he discovered that the island had been seized by the tyrant Polycrates during his absence. In Croton, he founded a community that became known for its strict dietary laws, dedication to mathematics and mystical contemplation of the cosmos.

That there was a real Pythagoras, now lost in time, might actually be supported by the very myths that accrued to him. Consider once again the fixation with food. Beans are a constant feature of these fables, prompting the question: why beans? He is said to have objected to them for practical reasons, namely as a cause of flatulence; for aesthetic reasons, because they look like testicles; for theological reasons, because they are like the gate of Hades – the ancient Greek underworld that Pythagoras was said to have visited; for political reasons, because beans are used in elections and elections lead to oligarchies; and for medical reasons, because they 'partake most of the breath of life'. What a wonderful euphemism for breaking wind.

Beans were the undoing of Pythagoras too. According to one account of his end, he was in a house meeting with his followers, when one Cylo, a local autocrat whom Pythagoras had slighted, set fire to the building. Pythagoras' disciples were nothing if not loyal, perhaps as a result of the hurdles they had to leap during their training to be his followers. They formed a protective barrier for their master, badly burning themselves. He escaped. Almost free, he reached a field in which beans were growing. This he refused to cross. As a result, Cylo's thugs caught up with him, cut his throat and left him to die. Maybe an obsession with pods and seeds, written in blood, is the most reliable fact we have about him.

Whatever the history, it is clear is that the figure of Pythagoras became an object of fascination for many different groups of people. The ancient Romans celebrated him as a philosopher and claimed him as their own, because he had lived on Italian soil. The aesthetic-loving souls of the Renaissance associated him with the personified *Musica* because he supposedly discovered the link between music and mathematical intervals whilst fiddling around on a monochord: if you halve the length of a string, the note, when plucked, rises by the perfect interval of an octave.

The Pythagoreans thought that mathematics was a necessary step towards unpeeling mere appearances, towards seeing the value of things. In its symmetries and patterns, calculus conveyed deep truths about reality. Numbers are in some way transcendent: one plus one would equal two regardless of whether we existed or not, or even whether the universe existed. Hence, it was said that when Pythagoras discovered his famous theorem, it seemed obvious to find an altar and sacrifice an ox. A window onto the world of the gods had been granted to humanity. He had seen something of the meaning of things.

Plato himself did much to keep alive the Pythagorean idea that mathematics lies at the basis of everything we can know about the universe. In one of his most Pythagorean moments, writing the dialogue *Timaeus*, Plato averred:

> The vision of the day and night and of months and circling years has created the art of number. It has given us not only the notion of time, but also the means of studying the nature of the universe, from which has emerged all philosophy in all its ranges.

In Plato's *Republic*, mathematics is described as kindling an organ in the soul that is worth a thousand 'normal eyes' because it is a deeper way of seeing the truth. It clarifies things. The ancient mathematician might be thought of as like a master carpenter: using mathematical tools – a setsquare and angle guide – to forge something of real beauty.

Such arguments have provided an imaginative and longlasting impetus in science. The astronomer Johannes Kepler referred to Pythagoras as 'grandfather of all Copernicans'. Galileo believed that the entire universe 'is written in the language of mathematics'. Bertrand Russell said that 'Mathematics, rightly viewed, possesses not only truth, but supreme beauty – a beauty cold and austere, like that of sculpture.' We are all Copernicans now. But are we all Pythagoreans too? Do we still believe that meaning can be founded upon mathematics – even for those of us who realised at school that maths was not their métier – and by analogy, extended to other parts of life?

Most contemporary mathematicians, for example, when they prove a theorem, go to the pub to sink a pint, not to the temple to sacrifice an ox. And yet, the Pythagorean vision of mathematics has never quite died. If the sales of books popularising mathematics are anything to go by, then the beauty of mathematics is still compelling. One of the authors of those books, Marcus du Sautoy, the professor for the public understanding of science at Oxford University, said this: 'I get my spiritual buzz out of the eternity of this [mathematical] world.' What did he mean? Well, consider this.

It's a question that most physicists must whisper to themselves from time to time. It was famously posed by a Nobel Prize winning physicist, Eugene Wigner, in 1960, when he wrote an essay entitled 'The Unreasonable Effectiveness of Mathematics in the Natural Sciences'. He was asking why mathematics works at all, when it comes to describing what happens in the world. It is, when you think about it, quite remarkable that the green leaves on a tree grow like a fractal pattern or that the force of gravity, which holds the planets in their places, falls off in a strict proportion to distance. Add to that the sense shared by most mathematicians that mathematics is not created, it is discovered. Doing maths is like exploring a foreign country, one that spreads out before you to be charted and traversed. Wigner writes: 'It is … a miracle that in spite of the baffling complexity of the world, certain regularities in the events could be discovered.' In his essay, he ponders what this 'unreasonable effectiveness' might mean.

The implication is that without understanding why and how

the mathematics works, neo-Pythagoreans might be justified in concluding that qualities like order and beauty – the qualities associated with mathematics – are written through the fabric of the universe. Moreover, if mathematics is discovered, not created, then perhaps to do mathematics is to uncover these things as well.

Such considerations lead some believers to call on mathematics as evidence for the existence of God – or to put it in a more nuanced way, they say that the power of mathematics is exactly the kind of thing you would expect in a universe created by an ordered and beautiful deity. The philosopher Leibniz wrote: 'When God calculates and thinks things through, the world is made.' For the theist, the belief is that human beings can apprehend God's 'thinking through' by doing maths. The physicist Michel Heller, who is also a priest, writes in his book, *The Comprehensible Universe*:

In the human brain, the world's structure has reached its focal point: the structure of the world has acquired the ability to reflect upon itself … In this conceptual setting, science appears as a collective effort of the Human Mind to reach the Mind of God … The Mind of Man and the Mind of God are strangely interwoven.

That is the thought of a neo-Pythagorean. It reaches back to the mystic from Samos. However, it is surely a fallacy to take mathematics as proof for the existence of God. For one thing, it is a big leap to go from the metaphysics of mathematics to the God of Abraham, Isaac and Jacob. Mathematics is not personal. And no-one would suggest you worship mathematics, for all that it may inspire awe.

In fact, the Pythagorean suggestion to us is more subtle. There is a power in mathematics that is intimately linked to qualities that provide human beings with their sense of meaning. And yet, the nature of that power remains something of a mystery. People are perfectly within reason to conclude that it doesn't say much about the existence of God at all. After all, one plus one equals two not because some god says so, but because it does. The mathematician John von Neumann put it this way: 'In mathematics you don't understand things. You just get used to them.' Alternatively, the biologist Richard Dawkins, a compelling advocate of atheism to many, finds no less cause to wonder at the order of things: 'The complexity of living organisms is matched by the elegant efficiency of their apparent design.' He argues that nature itself finds a way of climbing what he has called 'mount improbable', and it is no less remarkable for that.

Exactly what you make of mathematics is probably a question of your personal faith, or lack of it. The puzzle of Wigner's miracle, and Pythagorean geometry is, in a way, the same: at the end of the day, we don't know why there are laws, why mathematics works or why we can discover much about the universe at all. But the point is that we can. Moreover, there is something beautiful about it. The intuition that the world is a meaningful place for we humans is right. The figure of Pythagoras reminds us that science, far from undermining that sensibility, can in fact underpin it.

CHAPTER 2

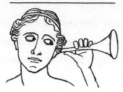

Sappho and the art of paying attention

If human beings are meaning-seeking creatures, there is another quality, related to it, which is important to highlight early on in our return to the ancients. In a word, it is this: curiosity. For if truly to believe that the world is a meaningless place is to commit yourself to an empty and pointless existence, then to lose all curiosity about life is to put quite a damper on it too. A sad world-weariness would be the result. More positively, to be curious about things is to cultivate a zest for life. The historian G.M. Trevelyan once remarked that intellectual curiosity is 'the life-blood of real civilisation'. Or you might note that questioning is close to questing, and questing, in turn, makes for a sense of purpose.

But curiosity is a virtue that can turn on you. In the proverb it killed the cat, and to overdo it would be to form the habits of a nosey-parker or, worse, inculcate a pervasive sense of restlessness: nothing the perennially dissatisfied person can find will ever satisfy them. So how can it be nurtured so as to ensure it is most productive of life? Where is the right balance? Sappho is our guide here. For her, a constructive curiosity is all about paying attention. It is a careful art requiring humility, patience and intelligence.

She stands out on any list of the wise from antiquity. Her profile rises not just because she was a woman – there were others – but because her work survives in her own words. And they are arresting words. She is the most clearly defined female figure from ancient Greece.

She was a poet, and famous in her own time. Her verse was almost lost during the medieval period, though just enough fragments made it through history for us to have a clear sense of her voice, and so celebrate her once again.

> Some say a host of horses, some say an army of infantry,
> and some say an army of ships is the most beautiful thing
> on the black earth. But I say it is whatever one loves.

She was born on the Ionian island of Lesbos, a place long associated with art and verse. Arion, who invented an ancient Greek form of ecstatic verse, originated from the same large isle. Legend has it that he was rescued from pirates by its dolphins. Terpander, the founder of Greek music, lived there too, a generation before Sappho.

This lyrical history subsequently gained a momentum of its own. Even my guidebook says that Lesbos 'hangs off the coast of Turkey like a gingko leaf'. It continues:

> Its vineyards produce Greece's best ouzo, its undulating
> hills support an astonishing 13 million olive trees, while
> the higher peaks are swathed with chestnuts and pines
> … the islanders are easygoing, lyrical and fond of horses
> and drink, ready to break into song or dance whenever
> the mood takes them. Music and poetry run deep in
> Lesbos' soul, and contribute to its well-known bewitch-
> ing quality.

Figure 4 *Sappho and Alcaeus* by Lawrence Alma-Tadema. Alcaeus, another lyric poet, described her as 'violet-haired, holy, sweetly smiling'

Sappho made her substantial contribution to the tradition associated with her birthplace around the turn of the seventh century BCE. This was at the same time as the forerunners of ancient Greek philosophy were beginning to emerge, about a century before Socrates. It might seem odd to associate her with philosophy now, for all that it did not seem strange to the philosophers that followed her. So why did they value her, and what has that to do with curiosity?

Plato himself is said to have called Sappho wise. There is an epigram attributed to him which goes: 'Some say the Muses are nine: how careless! Look, there's Sappho too, from Lesbos, the tenth.' It is the association with the muses that makes for the association with wisdom. They were regarded as the inspirers of the yearning that leads to learning. The word itself echoes with the practice of thought, as in 'musing'. Similarly, in mythology, the muses were the daughters of Zeus and Mnemosyne, the goddess of memory. It seemed perfectly natural for Shakespeare to call upon the tenth muse, Sappho, to pour into his verse 'thine own sweet argument'.

There is another dimension to this particular kind of wisdom to draw attention to. She is remembered as a poet of love. As the name Lesbos implies, she is particularly associated with the love of women for women. Whether or not she was a lesbian in the modern sense is a moot point. She could portray, and presumably felt, passion for men too. What was so remarkable to her contemporaries was not the objects of her desire but the way she could conjure it up. They felt that desire in themselves merely from reading her words. She was called a 'wonderful phenomenon': her technical accomplishment was noted; her aesthetic was appreciated and replicated; the power of her words took the breath away.

Eros shook my mind like wind falling on oaks down the mountain.

That is a beautiful image.

She must have struck those around her as so remarkable for another reason too; for the first time they could read about love from the woman's perspective. As a rule, ancient Greeks saw women not as different from men but as less than men. Aristotle had a theory that women were born when, during gestation, there had not been enough heat in the womb. This understanding of biology is objectionable to us, though there is a consolation in it, since it implies that there is no intrinsic gulf between men and women, as if one were from Mars, the other Venus. That noted, the logic of it is that if you want to know about what it is to be human you should turn to the most perfectly formed specimens. Men would eclipse anything that women could contribute, or so it was supposed.

Sappho is one of the first to challenge that assumption, to

question it, not by taking issue with the biology, but by demonstrating otherwise. This is where her curiosity comes in. Imagine what it would have taken. Perhaps she had to be brave, though there are no indications that she was ever at personal risk; it is likely that she was commissioned to write for public festivals and parties, so there is no sense in which she worked underground. But she did have to find a new language for her feeling, a different grammar for her sex. Generating feminine imagery in a poetic world that was dominated by the masculine and military metaphors of Homer was an enormous undertaking. Her literary innovation is the basis for her admirable genius. She changed perspectives and thereby minds.

> I would rather see her sexy walk and the shining sparkle
> of her face than Lydian chariots or armed infantry.

Set against a culture of pomp and ceremony, there is a tremendous honesty in that verse. Her ability to set down on the page

Figure 5 Bust of Sappho, Roman copy of fifth-century BCE original

feelings that were usually suppressed must have delighted her admirers.

Alternatively, in another fragment, she daringly inverts the *casus belli* of the Trojan war. It was not that Helen was stolen by Paris, the traditional reason given for the brutal conflict, but that she went of her own accord:

> Easy to make this entirely understood by all. For Helen, who surpassed mortals by far in beauty, left her noble husband and went sailing to Troy.

Behind this audacity lay the quality that makes her wise, namely her capacity to pay close attention to things. She could see the world differently, through a woman's eyes, because she was curious about the world around her. That is harder to do than it might first seem. Today, philosophers and biologists alike tell us that our perceptions of the world come to us already shaped; we interpret the world in the way we do because of our evolutionary or cultural inheritance. Objects, bodies, moods do not come to us naked or innocent but as particular kinds of objects, bodies and moods, preloaded with meaning and significance – or loaded down with meaning and significance, the artist might say, when trying to attach different meanings to things. Sappho was able to pay such close attention to objects, bodies and moods that she managed to imagine them in a different way. She broke free from the preconceptions of her day, and so found a freedom for herself. 'Poetry is eloquent painting,' thought Simonides, one of Sappho's successors. It is an analysis that could be stripped down even further to say 'art is seeing', seeing as if for the first time. That might be a good definition for the virtue of curiosity we are seeking.

One of the most famous fragments, number 31, demonstrates

how Sappho paid attention, in this case in relation to emotion.
Here it is in full:

> He seems to be to be equal to the gods, that man, who-
> ever sits opposite you and listens to you speaking so
> sweetly and close to him, and hears too your tempting
> laughter. Truly that makes the heart in my breast pound,
> for when for a moment I look at you, I cannot speak at all;
> my tongue breaks, and a subtle flame runs immediately
> beneath my skin. My eyes see nothing at all and a roaring
> fills my ears. Sweat pours down me, and shaking seizes
> me all, paler than grass I am, and little short of dead I
> seem to me. But all must be endured since ...

Notice what happens. Sappho begins conventionally enough,
noting the handsome man:

> He seems to be to be equal to the gods, that man, who-
> ever sits opposite you and listens to you speaking so
> sweetly and close to him, and hears too your tempting
> laughter.

But even in that one sentence, our attention has been turned
from him to she who sits opposite, speaking sweetly and laughing alluringly. It is this spectacle that absorbs Sappho's awareness, and she continues:

> Truly that makes the heart in my breast pound, for when
> for a moment I look at you, I cannot speak at all; my
> tongue breaks, and a subtle flame runs immediately
> beneath my skin.

There is a lovely paradox here. She cannot speak and yet words
capture that feeling so well. Attraction is like that, so commonplace that everyone knows it; so exceptional that when it

happens to you, you must imagine it as unique and astonishing. The woman who finds words – the woman who unlike the stereotype not only keeps thinking whilst she feels, but perceives all the more profoundly – goes on:

> My eyes see nothing at all and a roaring fills my ears.
> Sweat pours down me, and shaking seizes me all, paler
> than grass I am, and little short of dead I seem to me. But
> all must be endured since …

The result is a deeper insight again. The most striking is the reflection that love is like death. That which is most invigorating, filling the ears with its roar, feeling like a flame under the skin, is simultaneously that which is incapacitating. Death is the right association: the postcoital body collapses as if spent; ecstasy literally means stepping out of yourself, which would leave you as if dead. We have come a long way from the first image of the godlike man.

Sappho noticed nature too. For her contemporaries, she must have been a joy to read since she takes them directly to her enchanted island:

> [Come] here to me from Crete to this holy temple,
> where is your charming grove of apple-trees, and altars
> smoking with frankincense, and in it cold water sounds
> through apple branches, and the whole land is shadowed
> by roses, and from shimmering leaves sleep drops down;
> in it a meadow grazed by horses blooms with spring
>   flowers,
> and the winds blow gently.

At one level this fragment can be read as a traditional Greek invocation. It serves to conjure up the god who inhabited the grove with the sound of its words, as well as the smell of the

incense. However, scholars have noted how Sappho intro-
duces a novel element. She conjures up a sense of being in that
place yourself. Alfred Biese, in his seminal study, *The
Development of the Feeling for Nature in the Middle Ages and
Modern Times*, traces it back to Sappho. In her is found 'that
most individual of all expressions of feeling', namely subjectiv-
ity. With her, 'classic song now shewed the tender subjective
feeling for Nature'. Again, that takes penetrating attention, a
revolutionary shift in perspective.

From the boughs of trees to the bodies of lovers, Sappho pays
attention in her poems. In that, she finds a creative, intellectual
liberty. It is curiosity as a habit, with which to muse and grow
wise. Simultaneously, she reveals something to us of the effort-
ful art of paying attention. It was to become a key element in the
way of life advocated by the philosophers. It might commend
itself to us too. And if, like me, you feel too nervous to try writing a poem, there is nothing to stop you developing the habit of
looking afresh at the world.

CHAPTER 3

Plato and a love of conversation

Plato is our central figure, the man whose 'podcasts' – as we have called the dialogues that spread around the ancient Mediterranean world – secured a future for philosophy as a way of life. So let us push further into the significance of this choice of medium, for it is indeed a central part of his message. The dialogue conveys two crucial features of the approach to life he is commending. One is passion, the other is talk. In short, Plato is making the case for a deceptively simple formula: quality of life is directly proportional to the delight you can take in discussion. Committed conversation would be, for him, a central activity in the art of living.

It is said that the night before Socrates and Plato met, Socrates had a dream. In it, he was seated. A grey cygnet was nestling in his lap. All at once, the bird's plumage changed into the white glory of the adult swan. The creature let out a call – a loud, clear, pure note – and took to the air. Socrates awoke, wondering what it meant. The next day he met Plato and understood. Plato was the swan.

This is a story, though it must have lasted because it conveys so much about Plato the man, and in particular the first element we are exploring here, his driving passion.

It is symbolised in the loud call – the sheer delight of the adult swan rejoicing in his newfound vigour. In a short play, *Above the Gods*, the novelist and scholar Iris Murdoch captured something of the passion of Plato by portraying him in conversation with Socrates and his peers in ancient Athens. They are talking about the power of eros, and sublimating the sexual drive. Plato gets increasingly excited, until he rises to his feet and exclaims:

> You see, love is energy. The soul is a huge vast place, and lots of it is dark, and it's full of energy and power, and this can be bad, but it can be good, and that's the work, to change bad energy into good, when we desire good things and are attracted magnetically by them.

In another place, Murdoch wrote: 'Our life problem is one of the transformation of energy.' Plato would have agreed with that focus on energy, love and how to channel it for the best. He tried to show how in several of his dialogues. There are twenty-six surviving that can said to be his for sure. Six or so stand out as unrivalled masterpieces: *Apology*, *Theaetetus*, *Symposium*, *Phaedrus*, *Republic* and *Timaeus*. Two of those – *Symposium* and *Phaedrus* – are about love, how it shapes our lives and can transform them. Love features strongly in nearly all the others too. Plato, the lover of wisdom, was fundamentally a philosopher of love.

Actual love affairs are part of the mythology that surrounds him too. One group of ancient writers described how, at his conception, Plato's parents made love too violently, such was their passion. It's a bizarre story, but reads as if the writers were trying to explain why this question of love's energy so pressed upon Plato during his life. It was there from the moment of his conception.

Then, there are lists of his own affairs. One was reportedly with the youth, Aster, a budding astronomer. Plato supposedly wrote him this verse:

Star-gazing Aster, would I were the skies,
To gaze upon thee with a thousand eyes.

Another story was that he had a youthful affair with an older, beautiful woman called Archeanassa. Plato wrote the following to himself when he remembered the impact her love-making had upon him: 'O hapless ye who met such beauty on its first voyage, what a flame must have been kindled in you!'

Another aspect that we can discern about Plato the man has to do with his powerful presence. Stories quickly grew up around him which suggest that he was strikingly charismatic and had a radiant personality. The most dramatic of these tales raised the possibility that he had a semi-divine nature. We know that he was born in 427 BCE, and the myth is that the day of his birth was Apollo's birthday. At his birth, the story continues, bees flew down from the heavens and rested on his lips – the lips that were to engage in conversation as sweet to the ears as honey is to the tongue. The swan in Socrates' dream is itself the bird of Apollo.

This kind of talk sounds too extreme today, supernatural. And yet charismatic individuals are still described as scintillating – literally, emitting sparks or radiating white light. They are magnetic, exude an aura, have star quality. It is an elusive trait, not exactly to do with good looks but more with a look; not because they draw attention to themselves but perhaps because they are able to pay attention. They spontaneously evoke deeply emotional responses in others, often of adulation – though there is a risk that after such encounters, people can feel that the individual was playing with their emotions. That is the downside of projecting passion.

When I was at university, one of my lecturers had something of this effect on students. More and more people packed into the lecture room as his courses progressed, not so much to hear what he had to say, but rather for the experience. One day, whilst walking back to my college, I bumped into a friend and enthusiastically exclaimed that he too should not miss the talks. They were just too good. 'Well, what does he say?' my friend asked, slightly exasperated. When I thought about it, I couldn't quite relate the specifics. It was the love of ideas which was projected that moved and mattered.

Such presence echoes in another of the anecdotes about Plato that has been passed on. It is said that he started out as a wrestler. His success in this contact sport was due to his broad physique: he would have filled a room body as well as soul. The sport was possibly the origin of his name too, 'Plato' being a pun on the Greek for 'broad', *platus*. He was originally named Aristocles, after his grandfather, adopting the nickname later.

Changing your name is a significant thing to do. It reflects a desire to move on, unencumbered by the past. Or it can be a way of demonstrating that a corner has been turned, that you have indeed changed. Plato himself certainly believed in personal transformation. That is what he thought a love of encountering others in conversation could achieve, and much of his philosophy is aimed at evoking such shifts, probably because he had experienced such a conversion himself when he was twenty years old. A leading light amongst Athens' young literary stars – carrying the torch of Aeschylus, Sophocles and Euripides – he was about to compete for the great prize awarded at the festival of Dionysius. He had penned a tragedy. Only this was the morning after Socrates' dream. Plato came across him conversing in front of the theatre. They talked and his life changed. The swan took flight. Without a second thought, he burnt the work he'd written and which was about to be performed. He is said to have called out these words: 'Come hither, O fire-god, Plato now has need of thee.'

That was Plato's experience and he wanted to pass it on. To do so, he had to replicate the conditions that could produce the change when passionate minds meet. To put it another way, he had to think about education, and as a result he developed very particular ideas about it. They express more about this love of conversation.

Plato felt that a true education had to be done in person, ideally in a small group of people who displayed a commitment to

Figure 6 Socrates as depicted in the medieval Nuremberg Chronicle

each other. There was a common saying that did the rounds in ancient Athens: 'Friends hold all things in common.' Plato quotes it several times in his dialogues and it could have become a kind of motto for his philosophical method. Only with friends, he thought – a fellowship of loving trust – can individuals openly explore the complexities of their lives and how they relate to their convictions, their feelings, their hopes and their character. With friends, new ways of understanding and appreciating the world emerge, quite naturally. The daily interchange that friends enjoy, over long periods of time, during different stages of life, is the meat and drink of Plato's educational ideal. And it takes time too: in the *Republic*, one character says that any decent education takes five years to get going, and moreover, can only really begin when someone is over thirty-five years old – that is, when they have reached a certain level of general maturity.

Plato used to contrast his idea of learning by total immersion amongst friends with that of the more combative style of aggressive debate in which Athenians also engaged. He was sure that the latter approach just couldn't work. It only bolstered defensive positions and didn't open one person up to another:

> When two friends, like you and me, are in the mood to chat, we have to go about it in a gentler and more dialectical way. By 'more dialectical,' I mean not only that we give real responses, but that we base our responses solely on what the interlocutor admits that he himself knows.

It is sometimes said that metaphysics leads the individual by the hand towards the truth. Plato might have added that friendship is needed for such leading too.

Friends speak words, of course. But unlike the words on a page, which relate indirectly to life, face-to-face conversation – with its vulnerabilities and immediacy, its halts and flows – can be a direct expression of current reality. A life in common generates living words, penetrates secret thoughts, observes by example. The philosopher of conversation, Theodore Zeldin, has written:

> Conversation is a meeting of minds with different memories and habits. When minds meet, they don't just exchange facts: they transform them, reshape them, draw different implications from them, engage in new trains of thought. Conversation doesn't just reshuffle the cards: it creates new cards.

That dynamic was exactly what Plato was after.

There is a surviving snapshot of life in Plato's Academy, as he called his school of conversation, as seen through the eyes of the comic playwright, Epicrates. In it, Epicrates has a laugh at Plato's expense. He imagines the philosopher and his disciples studiously examining, discussing and contemplating the nature of a pumpkin:

> Well now, first of all they took up their places, and with heads bowed they reflected a long time.

This is how one of Epicrates' characters begins the description of what goes on in the school. He continues:

> Then suddenly, while they were still bent low in study, one of the lads said it was a round vegetable, another that it was a grass, another that it was a tree. When a doctor from Sicily heard this, he dismissed them contemptuously, as talking rubbish.

So striking was Plato's notion of a collective education that it caused much mirth amongst his contemporaries: what do those men and women – there were women in the school too – do all day, they joked? The friends who held all things in common could disagree, violently at times. We know they did. But it was precisely their commitment to this communal pursuit, the thing which Epicrates mocks, that was striking and which bound them together.

These philosophers were so linked that they wore the same clothes, a simple monkish cloak, and shared meals as readily as they shared their thoughts. Moreover, it was not just that Plato thought women could be educated, alongside men. He also argued that an education required people to be treated equally and that they should be free. That too was vital for a true meeting of minds.

Figure 7 The site of Plato's Academy in Athens today (Photo: Tomisti)

The Academy was physically situated in a grove called Hekademos. It occupied the corner of a park, just outside the walls of the city. Sophists before Plato's time had been in the habit of meeting there, so it was quite natural for Plato to set up shop in the same spot during the early 380s BCE. Once established, Plato erected a shrine to the Muses in the grove, probably to signal what was going on since the site was outdoors and open to the public. Plato also had a private estate and house, and since he did not marry, he must have given that over to his life's work too.

It would have been extraordinary to have lived at the dawn of this new experiment in thinking and living, and to have been part of it. Plato was constructing a highly innovative way of life. Little wonder that the Academy attracted the most gifted individuals of the time. Aristotle attended for twenty years, as did the astronomer Eudoxos and the mathematician Theaetetus. In fact, that very success, and the increasing number of people he attracted, came to present Plato with a conundrum. Friendship, soul-searching and love were at the heart of it: 'Concepts are always dressed in emotions,' said another Plato scholar A.N. Whitehead. This means that being physically present is central to the ideal. A Platonic eduction was nothing if not an embodied activity. However, when you are successful, you must work out how to reach larger numbers, and somehow not dilute the core message. Plato's conundrum was how to square that particular circle. And it is via some reflections on the contemporary invention of the podcast that we might illuminate what he did next.

The contemporary philosopher Hubert Dreyfus can be our temporary guide here. He is in the enviable position of having his lectures, as podcasts, widely listened to online. On iTunes U, he is routinely in the top 20, and his lectures give a good showing in the general listings as well. This has led him to ponder the value of podcasts in education. Clearly they have some value, and reach audiences he never could in person. But they are not as valuable as attending a lecture course itself, of being physically engaged with other students at tutorials, of developing that love of conversation.

He believes that it is the risk, involvement and commitment of being physically present that makes the difference. It is because we have bodies that we feel in touch with the world. Similarly it is by being vulnerable to and present with others in conversation that we put ourselves in the best place to learn, discover and remember. It nurtures a kind of friendship.

This has led the professor to assemble a kind of scale of learning. It begins with being a novice, then comes the advanced beginner. After that someone reaches competence, then proficiency, next expertise and finally mastery. Roughly, disembodied learning, over the internet via podcasts, can get you through stages one and two – from novice to advanced beginner. But there on in, through competence and proficiency, and certainly when it comes to expertise and mastery, a fellowship of risk-taking and trust is the must-have environment.

So the compromise that Professor Dreyfus has reached is this: he happily puts podcasts, and webcasts, online. They are valuable means of introducing individuals to philosophy. However, he hopes that when people become serious about the subject, they will want to participate in a course.

Plato had access to a technology which though not entirely new, had recently been revived. That was writing. A very serious discussion was underway about the role that literature might play in education and for a long time Plato said he wouldn't write anything at all. In this, he was following the habit of his master, Socrates. 'Every serious man in dealing with really serious issues carefully avoids writing,' Plato warns in the *Seventh Letter* – the one ascribed to Plato that is generally thought to be his own.

The risks with writing are multiple, and run parallel to the limitations of the podcast. Writing is impersonal so people can't respond in person with questions, then receive answers, which leads to more questions, and so on. Alternatively, readers can misapprehend insights that can only truly be grasped after the total immersion training that comes when living a carefully designed way of life with others. You have to be in the right place ethically and existentially to receive wisdom, not only be able to read. Plato had a point: if reading were enough, the number of wise individuals in the world would be directly proportional to the number of books in the world. That does not appear to be the case.

Plato believed that philosophy is not the kind of knowledge that can be transmitted; it is not like water that can be poured from jar to jar, as he puts it in one dialogue. The kind of understanding he is after is more like a seed that takes time to germinate and grow, and will only do so in a nurturing environment. It is about honing desires rather than rational descriptions. Philosophy as a way of life is ultimately not about facts and proofs, but values and change. The practise makes perfect.

But many, many people were drawn by Plato's charisma, his ideas, and his success. How could he cope with the demand?

Probably late in his life, Plato changed his mind about writing. He was persuaded to compose dialogues and distribute the manuscripts. 'Written discourse goes rolling around in every direction,' he mused wryly, acknowledging the downside too. A life of Plato, written soon after he died, judged his experiment as follows: 'By composing his dialogues, he exhorted a mass of people to do philosophy; but he also gave many the opportunity to do philosophy in a superficial way.' The same could be said of the podcast.

And yet, the dialogue form was a canny choice for Plato to make. For one thing, it was popular. There is evidence that people of the time greatly enjoyed reading such discursive exchanges of ideas, as people love to load up their iPods. And for another, dialogues also carried an implicit warning: they presented real people engaged in argument, showing their emotions as well as playing their intellectual best hand. They stressed the need for interaction and embodiment. (Perhaps this is why the most engaging podcasts capture the presence of the lecturer too, or are in the form of a conversation.) They were a kind of testimony to Plato's educational ideal: a love of conversation. It is as if Plato were writing a warning into the very structure of what he produced: do not read as a treatise! – though, of course, they are routinely treated as such today.

The dialogues he produced vary in style, difficulty and subject, as if he were attempting to reach different audiences. Some seem suited to the intelligent layman. Others engage specialist language and so seem designed as interventions in scientific and theological disputes. Others again read like summaries of debates that would have taken place in the Academy; they are model discourses around which students could shape their own exchanges. The different genres merge into one another too. It is part of their genius that they can be read by anyone, drawing them in to explore deeper and deeper reflections. For behind the dialogues, Plato insisted, was what he called an 'unwritten teaching', that which can only be manifest in a life.

So you can say that the dialogues are invitations to do philosophy, introductions to lead you towards competence and entice you to desire proficiency, expertise and mastery. A dialogue can inform you. However, only conversation in the flesh, with others, powered by your passion, can reform you – can transform you into a philosopher.

Here, then, is a third tip for good living that comes from the ancients. It is Plato's conviction that the well-lived life is found in the delights of discussion. We must converse with one another. It is an insight that we may put into practice in seminars and studies during our student years. But if Plato is right, we must carry the habit out into the rest of life, and make life itself a kind of school.

Plato was not the only person to write dialogues in his time. There was an explosion of interest in the genre. Similarly, today, the growth of the internet – of podcasts, blogs and the like – can be taken as evidence that people love to communicate, and often convey their passion when so doing. However, Plato would say, don't forget the communal dimension. It is equally crucial. Rhetoric that mostly seeks to defeat perceived opponents may advance a cause but it doesn't much advance human wisdom. Friendship and commitment are key, because they make it possible for the individual to take the risks that can lead to a transformation of his or her life.

CHAPTER 4

Diogenes the Cynic on the deceptiveness of fame

Paris Hilton famously became famous by distributing on the internet a video of herself having sex with her then boyfriend, Rick Salomon. She was born into copious wealth, as heir to the Hilton hotel dynasty – though it seems she might have lost that revenue stream after being disinherited by the patriarch of the family, who was offended by her shamelessness online. And yet, the cash didn't count. It was currency of a different sort that Paris desired; that cultural currency called fame.

By that, she did not mean the easy renown she could enjoy by being an 'It-girl', embodying the glamour of the bright young things who move in society circles. Neither did she want the transient fifteen minutes of fame allotted to mortals by Andy Warhol. It had to be bigger. The sex tapes secured it. They launched her career as someone who had not just fame but 'vfame', to use the word coined by Mark Rowlands in his book *Fame* – new variant fame, fame for being famous, named after vCJD, the brain-rotting disease.

But should we be bothered about the vfame of characters like

Paris, and what the fame we afford her might say about us? Surely it is enough just to think that the fame of the few is harmless, merely generating a supply of distractions to pass the time of day for the many who remain obscure. After all, no-one actually believes that the famous are better, unless someone of renown has done something remarkable to deserve it – which itself would be quite remarkable these days.

There was an ancient philosopher who can help us think about this facet of modern life. He apparently deployed sex in public as a strategy for commanding attention too. He was called Diogenes, lived in the fourth century BCE and founded a school of philosophy called the Cynics. The label comes from the Greek for dog: Diogenes became so famous that throughout ancient Greece he was known simply by the single word 'Dog'. Having a monomial name is, of course, the key sign that you've really made it, like 'Paris'.

Figure 8 *Diogenes* by Jean Leon Gerome

The seeming similarities between Paris and Dog do not stop
there. He was also born into money. Hicesias, his father, was a
banker in Sinope, an important trading city in what is now
northern Turkey on the Black Sea. The city stood half way
between the Hellespont and the Causasus. If you arrived there,
perhaps on a merchant ship carrying olive oil from the
Mediterranean, and disembarked at its harbour, you could
travel south inland and discover that it was encircled by that
timeless source of wealth, vast fields of wheat.

Bankers thrive on trade, and Hicesias was well placed to do
well: he worked at the city's mint. Until, that is, something
went wrong. He was prosecuted, and then exiled, for defacing
the coinage with which he was entrusted. In fact, the rumour
was that Diogenes himself had struck the faces off the money.
He had apparently received a message from the Delian oracle,
agent of the god Apollo. It said he should 'alter the political currency'. Displaying the disdain for cash that only rich kids can,
he understood the words of Apollo literally and debased the
coins, putting them out of circulation. Later, the oracle's message was to take on a more subtle meaning for him: he was to
challenge the polity of his day.

His father disgraced, Diogenes was destitute, though he
managed to make his way to Athens. According to the tradition, he found his first teacher there, Antisthenes. Antisthenes
had an excellent pedigree as he had been a close friend of
Socrates. He taught in the Cynosarges, a well-known gymnasium, a place where individuals could go to exercise and talk.
This one was for those who were not full citizens of Athens, or
who were the children of slaves, as Antisthenes was. The name
of the gymnasium means white or swift dog, after a legend that
on the site a canine had once snatched a lavish sacrifice of
meat being offered by a pious Athenian. The significance of the

theft is lost in the mists of time. That Diogenes learnt how to practise philosophy in 'the place of the white or swift dog' might have leant him the name for his school, the Cynics.

What did he learn? In short, the simple life – though a rather different simple life from the one depicted in Paris' TV show that went by the same name. It is said that one day Diogenes saw a mouse running about. It struck him how uninhibited the rodent was. It worried neither about where it might sleep, nor about what it might eat, nor did it seem scared of things like the dark. From that day on, Diogenes too would seek self-sufficiency by not having a care. In token of that, he once saw a child drinking water out of his hands and immediately threw away his own cup, shamed that a child should outdo him in frugality. Alternatively, whilst trying to find somewhere to live in his adopted city, the task became so wearisome that he took up residence in a barrel that he found outside a temple in the marketplace. This is perhaps the most famous of the arresting habits he adopted. Others apparently included rolling in baking-hot sand in the summer, and embracing stone-cold statues in the winter. He wanted to ensure that no hardship could take him by surprise.

Dogfights with other philosophers, who had become as common as foxes in the city, seem to have been a favourite pastime of Diogenes. On more than one occasion he declared that Plato's lectures were a vainglorious waste of time, not so much a love of conversation as a pure indulgence. To make his point, he would show up during intricate disputations at the Academy, Plato's school, waving a plucked chicken – in mockery of Plato's definition of man as a 'featherless biped'. Plato retorted that Diogenes was 'Socrates gone mad', adding that to accuse someone else of being vainglorious is a sure sign of your own pride. (That, though, prompts the question of whether accusing someone of being proud because they accuse you of being vainglorious is itself a sign of your pride.)

Diogenes' reputation grew as someone who chastised the people. He would stand in the marketplace and whistle, and a crowd would gather round him, like dogs. However, when he discussed something serious, they showed no interest and returned to their menial tasks. That earned them his scorn. In a similar vein, he noted that literary sorts loved to identify what was wrong with Homer, whilst remaining ignorant of their own failings. Or that musicians could tune the strings of a lyre, whilst their own lives were discordant. He condemned gluttons, the avaricious, the scheming. Perhaps unsurprisingly, he was one day beaten up by some youths – though he had the last laugh. When they'd gone, he wrote their names on a tablet, hung it around his neck and kept it there for so long that the ruffians themselves became objects of public ridicule. The foolish make fools of the world.

There were other ways in which Diogenes ribbed his contemporaries. He was once invited to dinner but refused to go because, he said, the last time his host had not expressed gratitude to him for coming. He was asked whether he believed in the gods, to which he replied that the god-forsaken wretches all around him demonstrated that Zeus and his companions must be real. Another time he lit a lamp in the middle of the day and, like a performance artist, walked around telling people he was searching for an honest human.

He also aimed his wrath at the powerful, and that won him a popular following. He called the politicians of his day the 'lackeys of the people'. When he was captured by Philip II after the humbling of Athens at the battle of Chaeronea, the King of

Macedon asked him who he was. 'A spy upon your insatiable greed,' he replied with aplomb – and was promptly freed.

King Philip's son was Alexander the Great, which leads to the best known story about Diogenes. Now himself king, and as a result of his conquests the most famous man on the planet, the ruler of the world came to see Diogenes. He happened to be in Corinth. Perhaps Alexander had heard how the philosopher had dealt with his father. That would have interested him because his relationship with the old man was nothing if not Freudian and complex. In fact, some said Alexander literally had a hand in Philip's death. So if Macedon Senior had been chastened by his confrontation with the sage, how would Junior fare? He found the Cynic, sunning himself. Alexander stood before him, casting Diogenes in his shadow, and declared: 'Make a request!' Diogenes barked: 'Stand out of my sun!' Junior was humbled with a snarl too.

The people of Athens showed their respect for the one who was prepared to snap at the heels of their masters when one day Diogenes' barrel was destroyed by a lout. They beat the youth, and clubbed together to buy Diogenes another one.

Critic of the great. Oddity for the masses. But what was Diogenes' 'Paris moment'? When did he have sex in public?

Lewdness had already become an established part of his rhetorical routine. An effeminately dressed youth approached him; Diogenes demanded to see the cross-dresser's genitalia. He saw another young man lounging louchely in the marketplace, unwittingly exposing himself. 'Up, man, up, lest some foe thrust a dart in your back,' Diogenes yelled. At a dinner party, he became the butt of his fellow diners' jokes and they kept throwing him bones, as they would have done to a dog. Following their lead, Dog stood up and peed over them.

However, his *pièce de résistance* was this: masturbating in public.

The occasion on which he pleasured himself in the sun was apparently prompted by a shortage of cash: he hadn't been able to buy food and was hungry. Thus, when his right hand had completed the job, he remarked that he wished it were as easy to relieve the pangs in his stomach by rubbing his belly.

The action greatly enhanced his celebrity. As a result, he became one of the most cited philosophers in antiquity. One hundred years later, Chrysippus, then head of the Stoics, praised Diogenes for this action. Two hundred years after that, Philodemus, whose library was entombed in the lava of Herculaneum, again recalled what had happened, though this time to condemn it. The fathers of the early Christian church were similarly nonplussed. But what can we make of it today? Does it suggest that fame, after all, might be the way to go?

Diogenes had a serious point. He did not, in fact, have sex with someone he loved to win notoriety. He knew that he would become notorious for being outrageous, but unlike the vfamous, he was not outrageous in order to become notorious. Rather, the Dog was rejecting the conventions, beliefs and customs of his day in the most forthright way he could imagine. As an alternative, he advocated living according to nature, insofar as that is possible. He is better compared with the eco-warrior who wears dog-eared clothes, than the celebrity whose appearance has become as far from natural as is humanly possible whilst still remaining alive. Or think of the anarchist who rejects political dogma in the hope of finding ways to be free.

Diogenes the Cynic was remembered because of the strenuous demands of his way of life. He was a prophet, sparing no efforts to pass judgement on his times. What is the most beautiful thing in the world?, he was once asked. He replied:

'freedom of speech.' And that is hard to do well. The later philosopher, Epictetus, commented that the calling of the Cynic is beyond most people because it is too exacting. Epictetus idealises Diogenes to a degree, extolling his charm and appeal as well as his physical and mental toughness. The Cynic must be supremely virtuous, Epictetus continues, lest his or her censure of others' vices leave him or her open to the charge of hypocrisy. Cynicism is a vocation, and, Epictetus adds, Cynics are called to call out to others:

> O people, where are you bound? O miserable ones, what are you doing? You reel up and down, like the blind. You have left the real path and are going off on another one. You are looking for serenity and happiness in the wrong place, where it does not exist, and you do not believe when someone shows you. Why do you seek it in externals? It does not exist in the body.

So when Alexander stood before Diogenes, and Diogenes asked him to move, he was saying this: fame does not bring life – though Alexander bestrode the world in the hope of it. The sun does, and that everyone has. Fame is a fool's game, would be his judgement of Paris, though in fact he chose to become foolish.

Diogenes practised his liberty to the end. And it was these deeds that secured his fame, not any glory. His fellow citizens honoured him by erecting bronze statues, on which they inscribed these verses:

> Time makes even bronze grow old: but thy glory, Diogenes, all eternity will never destroy. Since thou alone didst point out to mortals the lessons of self-sufficingness and the easiest path of life.

So, if it is an expected conclusion to state that Diogenes does not endorse fame for fame's sake, there is a more subtle point his life makes too: when used to alleviate status anxiety or boredom, or even to make some noise around a genuinely worthy message, fame is still ephemeral and deceptive. The reason is that the strategy puts the cart before the horse. Instead, Diogenes says, work simply and solely on your message, your product or best of all on yourself. If your convictions are strong enough to shape your way of life, and you can make your own mind up, speak freely and set a lead, then that way of life will itself come to be worthwhile. Moreover, you can be sure that people will want to know about it.

CHAPTER 5

Diotima of Mantinea on sometimes not having sex

Diotima of Mantinea was arguably the greatest catalyst for erotic inspiration and spiritual passion in the history of Western culture, and yet today she is virtually unknown. In her day, she was acknowledged as an expert in the art of loving. Now, her very existence is doubted: scholars prefer to think of her as a muse of Plato's imagination – for it is in Plato's writings that she figures – though it is perfectly plausible to believe that she was an historical person of some influence.

Her voice would have been entirely lost to us were it not for Plato's tour de force, the *Symposium*, his most influential dialogue on love. This text arguably outshines Paul's letter to the Corinthians, John's gospel on Jesus, perhaps Shakespeare's sonnets and Freud's theories for the impact it has had on our ideas of love. In it are first uttered what have become commonplaces about affairs of the heart. We find the idea that romance is a search for your other half, or that love is a ladder that lifts you higher. It explores the treacherous links between loving and learning. It takes the cliché that love is blind and makes it into a project for life.

And yet, in the work that is routinely described as his poetic masterpiece, Plato doesn't speak at all. He is both silent and absent. He doesn't even allot the best lines to Socrates, his usual ploy for throwing his ideas into the ring. They are all given to Diotima. So what might she say to us?

She was born around 470 BCE, and died about sixty years later. The *Symposium* recounts a drinking party in 416 BCE during which its participants discuss the great matter of love. She was not present, and instead we hear about her through Socrates, who recounts meeting her when they were both much younger. It was with Diotima, he recalls, that he first really learnt about love. It was Diotima, he continues, who told him not just why people love, or what people want from love, but how love can penetrate the clouds of human ignorance and delusion to enable what can only be described as enlightenment.

Who is this remarkable woman, she whom Plato would have us believe spoke of mysteries that even wise Socrates had not understood? Socrates describes her as astute and shrewd, not only on matters of love but many other things as well.

Mantinea itself is a town situated in the central Peloponnese, the region known as Arcadia. A few years before the year in which Plato's *Symposium* is set, it had been the site of a great battle of the Peloponnesian war; Athenian armies were beaten and routed by their longstanding enemies the Spartans. The place would not have had positive associations for Socrates and his peers; it would have carried echoes of hate, not love. Diotima's reputation, though, had been fixed before that bloody event. She was a priestess and something of a wonder-worker: she apparently had a notable success when she correctly instructed the Athenians in the kind of sacrifice required to prevent the plague. Her preventative kept disease out for a decade.

Socrates doesn't say much about how he came to meet Diotima, only that it was she who taught him the 'arts of love'. That may imply that they were literally lovers, perhaps that Socrates lost his virginity to Diotima. Whatever the truth of that, it seems that he sought her out because he'd heard she knew something about love in a deeper sense – what love promises, how to nourish it, how it shapes human lives.

He himself had something of a reputation for seeking out wise women in pursuit of his fascination with love. There is another story, more notorious than his liaison with Diotima, that was frequently told in antiquity. One day, he visited Theodote, a famous courtesan, which is to say, a woman who was not a common prostitute but a veritable maestro of love. Men travelled long distances to learn from her body, and in return showered her with gifts; she lived in a splendid house.

The story goes that Theodote and Socrates launched into a conversation about her 'friends' and the 'favours' she gave them. At first, Theodote assumed that Socrates had come to her seeking satisfaction for his libidinal hungers too: she was in a state of voluptuous undress when he arrived, as she was sitting for a painter, and Socrates made the obvious comment about being aroused by the desire to touch her. However, the tables soon turned, when Theodote came to realise that Socrates roused unexpected desires in her – not because of his hand-some appearance, for he was ugly, but because of what he knew about love that she didn't. Socrates suggested that there is more to love than meets the eye, more than even Theodote had contemplated, the woman upon whom many eyes had rested. She ended up begging him to visit again and often, that she may benefit, body and soul. Socrates haughtily declined: she must come to him.

So what did Diotima teach Socrates? If you believe Plato, practically everything.

The key Greek word in all this is *eros*. Our word erotic, or sexual love, comes from it. However, the Greeks thought that erotic desire is a force that permeates life in all sorts of ways. When a hero in Homer strode out onto the battle field, he was said to be driven by *eros*, a desire to prove himself courageous. When a beautiful woman wept in the poems of Sappho, the cause of her suffering was *eros* because it awoke in her a love of impossible beauty. Plato imagined philosophical friendship cultivating such a *joie de vivre* that soulmates could sprout metaphorical wings and soar heavenwards, and they were inspired by *eros* too. So when Diotima promised to teach Socrates the art of erotics, she meant something far more than just how to be a good lover.

Eros is the cause of the initial attraction between lovers, though as they become more intimate and then confident in their relationship, it turns outward again, driving a renewed engagement with life. Echoes of *eros* can be heard in the later, distinctly Christian word for love too, *agape*, which is the overflowing love of God, a sort of universal benevolence: *eros* had divine as well as carnal overtones, and Eros was imagined by the Greeks as a god, or at least an intermediary between gods and men. This sense is perhaps most famously conveyed in Bernini's sensuous statue of Saint Theresa in ecstasy. The angel as Eros or Cupid stands above her, plunging his dart into her. It is union with God this loving brings.

The wealth of experience and possibility that is powered by love is reflected in other parts of the *Symposium*. The dialogue as a whole consists of the speeches made about love at the drinking party. The first is given by a character called Phaedrus. He presents a Homeric view of love that finds its

Figure 9 *The Ecstasy of Saint Theresa* by Gianiorenzo Bernini

highest expression in the courage exhibited in self-sacrificial acts. This love is the 'greatest love' now honoured when remembering those who have died in war, greatest because they have laid down their lives for others. Phaedrus argues that soldiers inspired by this love would perform such heroic deeds that they might never know defeat. He was thinking of the ancient Sacred Band, the famous army whose strength lay in the fact that it was made up of pairs of lovers. It is a stirring vision of love that can rouse individuals to an exceptional nobility and to that extent excellent human lives. But it is limited because it rests on a militaristic code. It is the love of the barracks. War is a persistent feature of human existence but it is not one that we can now commend as the norm.

A second speech discusses how love differs from lust. It is given by Pausanius and he praises love that is permanent. In such committed relationships, love is of someone body and soul. By contrast, lust is that force which would simply have its way; it is sexual gratification. Pausanias discusses the various laws and attitudes that different Greek cities had towards relationships at the time. Some are entirely lax, and he condemns those as shameless. Others are fiercely strict, and he rebukes them for being stifling. The approach he praises is that of Athens. Here a complex etiquette has evolved according to which lovers court one another. These rituals serve to separate the loving wheat from the lustful chaff, Pausanias says, thereby nurturing the one and weeding out the other. This reads as a strikingly liberal attitude.

A different take again is one that can seem rather banal: 'All you Need is Love', in the words of John Lennon's song. The person who represents this approach to love is the third speaker, a character called Agathon. Like Lennon's lyrics, with rhetorical flourishes instead of a tune, Agathon never achieves much more than repeating the word. Love is youthful, beautiful and virtuous; wise, peaceful and poetic; healing, festive and just, he says. All this might be true. But the encomium lacks grit. Perhaps like much modern self-help, it ends up being not very illuminating about the arts of love because it is so relentlessly, exhaustingly, optimistic. That is something to learn too: that there is a dark side of love is what makes it so important to get right.

A further speech, by one Eryximachus, adopts what you might call a scientific approach to love. Eryximachus was a doctor and his advice rests upon a theory about the universe in which it is love that draws the world together and hate that causes it to split apart. So, by analogy, a good life is one that achieves the right physical and psychological balance. However, Eryximachus was probably the kind of person who would obsessively calculate the fat content of his meals. He also discusses the benefits of divination for putting you in touch with these cosmic ebbs and flows, so he could be thought of as a devotee of the New Age, a little uptight with superstitious hokum. His is the love of the beauty spa or astrology column, harmless enough in its place, we might conclude, though trite.

There are other reflections on the nature of love in Plato's discussion. One has the brilliant idea that love is searching for your lost half, made by the comic poet Aristophanes. However, to return to Diotima: Socrates confesses that he had not dissimilar ideas about love as his companions – fine but familiar, you might say – until, that is, he met her. Afterwards, his perspective completely changed; it was like an awakening.

She told him that love could be more than a happy relief from the otherwise lonely business of being a human individual, and more than one ingredient amongst others in the medley that makes up a good life, from the blessings of good health to good children. Love is at once more powerful and more alarming.

It is the desire that can carry you towards your highest aspirations, or plunge you into your deepest fears. It is what you love that you give yourself to, though it is what you love that you also dread losing the most. It can hone your character, or eat you up. It can awaken in you a yearning for that which is beautiful and good, as well as drive you towards that which is carnal and corrupt. Love can set you on a virtuous path that, once initiated, spirals towards intimations of transcendence, or fling you in a vicious spiral towards your doom. It is a ladder to heaven, and hell.

Diotima was a priestess and her vision of love is religious; like religion, love draws the best out of people and the worst. In ecstasy, it can lift people out of themselves and towards life in all its fullness. As an obsession, it can turn them in on themselves and even be a cause of death. One thing, though, is for sure. Once you have seen the full power of love, life can never look the same again. In that it is good.

The implication is that meeting Diotima was a revelation for Socrates. The effect she had on him could not have been more profound. Heroic love, cosmic love, lustful love, all you need is love: they all came to seem mean ways of talking about it. After Diotima, according to Plato, Socrates developed a completely new account of love. Presumably Theodote sensed this when Socrates came to call. She, who had thought of herself as a love expert, was totally taken by surprise. She was drawn to this magnificent vision, though she might well have drawn back from it too. For if love is such a tremendous force, for good and ill, then how can it be tamed, nurtured or controlled?

Diotima's answer would have troubled her rival. It was a question of sex, and Theodote, for all that she was classy, made her living from that. Diotima did not celebrate virginity or advocate celibacy, but she did think that when it came to sex, less is probably more. Sex is an energiser, it quickens desire, it is a first step. But sex should not be equated with love, because carnal pleasures are but an echo of spiritual delights; the love of the body is only one manifestation of the love of beauty. The great risk with sex is that it is so compelling, so full of promise, that people get hooked on it. So, Diotima advised, sometimes in life – perhaps for a period of time, a sabbatical – you should lay sex to one side. Its energy should be sublimated into the pursuit of a higher love, one that is less about possession and more about contemplation. That is her suggestion to us.

This rechannelling of the erotic captures the original meaning of the phrase 'Platonic love'. Properly speaking, a Platonic relationship is one that has transcended the purely sexual, and discovered a way of loving that seeks satisfactions elsewhere. The reduced meaning of Platonic love, as a relationship that has no erotic component at all, is not only unlikely in life but wrong as a matter of historical fact.

The erotics that Plato ascribes to Diotima have been very informative in the West. This is why it is fair to suggest that the words of this almost forgotten priestess have been such a great catalyst for erotic inspiration and spiritual passion. They inform the celibate life of monks and nuns, individuals who partly for practical reasons – to enable themselves to live happily in community – and partly for spiritual reasons – to free themselves to love God – renounce sexual relationships. 'Love chastity' says Saint Benedict in the Rule he devised for monastics, chastity being the commitment to shape your erotic life towards the love of God. He was taking up where Diotima and Plato left off.

In the medieval period, the notion of channelling erotic desire in nonsexual ways re-emerged in the phenomenon of courtly love. Courtly love was imagined as the affection a knight feels for his lady, an affection that does not seek its fulfilment in sex but in sacrifice. In fact, typically the knight would give himself to a woman who was beyond reach, perhaps because she was already married. It was the very impossibility of sexual fulfilment that would drive him to chivalrous feats. The Dutch historian Johan Huizinga describes it like this: 'It is sensuality transformed into the craving for self-sacrifice, into the desire of the male to show his courage, to incur danger, to be strong, to suffer and to bleed before his lady-love.'

Another variant on the theme is found in the Eastern traditions of tantra, as described in the *Kama Sutra*. 'Kama' is a word that signifies both sexual pleasure and spiritual fulfilment. The ultimate aim of this manual of love is not to teach erotic acrobatics but a union of souls; spiritual questing through sexual congress. Moreover, the *Kama Sutra* advises that if an obsession with sex is causing an individual to neglect other parts of his or her life, from the pursuit of good things such as wealth and friends to the desire for enlightenment, then he or she should refrain from it, take some time off.

That may seem like a drawback today, though Diotima would have argued that her advice is actually empowering. Does not sex commonly become less important in a relationship as it evolves from falling in love to standing in love? Don't thrills give way to intimacies, kicks to companionship? Self-help books might advise you to seek ways of spicing up your sex life, to inject it with a renewed sexual passion. Diotima would say that is a mistake because it is to misunderstand the nature of the erotic and actually to miss out on the best part. Instead, set your sights higher: rejoice that the energy you once spent in pursuit of the sensual can be released for more glorious things too.

CHAPTER 6

Aristotle on surviving unpopularity

Who in life would not like to be popular, to be loved, or just to be appreciated? Conversely, who would deliberately choose mockery over respect, loneliness over camaraderie, condemnation over admiration? It turns out that several ancient philosophers did. They made a virtue out of being despised – though, not all of those who found themselves so censured by their peers positively chose the predicament. In fact, the stories of the individuals who *involuntarily* ended up being derided by others are all the more arresting for that reason. They were unpopular through no particular fault of their own; they did not seek out contempt. Rather, it was a question of fate or bad luck. When the goddess Tyche – or Fortuna, as the Romans knew her – casts her lot against you, the blow can be heavy. It readily leads to a sense that life is futile. So the question becomes how some could suffer such a bad hand and not become bitter. When it comes to the art of living, that is a much more interesting matter to pursue.

Aristotle is our man here. Several times during his life, things seemed to unravel for him and he became very unpopular with his fellows. As a result, he spent no small part of his time hurriedly moving around the Mediterranean from city to city, searching for a safe haven. How did the animosity of others affect him? How did he survive it, if he did? Consider the story of his life.

In *The Canterbury Tales*, Geoffrey Chaucer tells of a clerk from Oxford. He is a meagre-looking fellow – 'hollow' and 'threadbare' – for the reason that he has spurned worldly success in favour of wise philosophy. He is particularly wedded to the thought of Aristotle:

> He would rather have at his bed's head,
> Some twenty books, all bound in black and red,
> Of Aristotle and his philosophy
> Than rich robes, fiddle, or gay psaltery.

It may have come as something of a surprise to Chaucer's Oxford clerk, therefore, to learn that Aristotle himself was

Figure 10 Aristotle as a philosopher, a Roman copy of an ancient Greek original (Photo: Giovanni Dall'Orto)

style-conscious, even showy, at least in his youth. 'His calves were slender, his eyes small, and he was conspicuous by his attire, his rings, and the cut of his hair.' So says Diogenes Laertius. One can only presume that the beard came later, after he had established himself as a sage.

Diogenes also tells us that Aristotle spoke with a lisp, an appealing personal detail to remember next time you're browsing his *Politics*, *Metaphysics*, *Ethics* or any other of the thirty irreplaceable books he authored that survive to this day. In his lifetime, he was known to have penned at least 150.

Other fragmentary details flesh out our picture of Aristotle as a wealthy, wise and worldly man. His first wife was called Pythias, and with her he had two sons. She died young and he married again. He had another son, Nicomachus, with his second wife, Herpyllis. He also had an adopted son, Nicanor. He felt that his followers and disciples were part of his family too. When he moved home, he resettled with them.

Aristotle's unpopularity stemmed from his involvement in high politics, low demagoguery and all round upheaval. Not that he deliberately chose his lot. We can pick up the story when he arrived in Athens in 367 BCE, at the age of seventeen, from his birthplace, the town of Stagira – an attractive settlement, set across two hills and overlooking a small headland. He came to Athens to sit at the feet of Plato, and was part of the Platonic circle for twenty years, first as a student at Plato's school and then as a teacher. It must have been a tremendous time: Plato and Aristotle's relationship would have been high-powered to say the least; two giants of intellectual history – one already established and celebrated, the other fresh and emergent.

So it is perhaps not surprising that when the split came, it was painful. Plato reportedly remarked: 'Aristotle spurns me,

Figure 11 Plato (centre left) and Aristotle (centre right) as depicted in Raphael's *The School of Athens*

as colts kick out at the mother who bore them.' The kicking colt set up his rival school, the Lyceum. He liked to walk as he taught, and his followers became known as the Peripatetics.

The differences between Aristotle and Plato were to have massive repercussions in the history of thought. They effectively gave birth to two ways of doing philosophy, Aristotle's more inclined to the practical and analytic, Plato's to the rational and speculative. This difference is what Raphael depicts in his famous picture of the two philosophers: he has Plato pointing to the heavens, Aristotle to the earth. You could sum it up by saying that if Plato was a natural theologian, Aristotle was a natural scientist. This explains why Aristotle is often preferred by materialists and atheists today, on the grounds that he is the more empirical of the thinkers. He observed the world and categorised it. And yet, the differences between the two can be overdone. It is easy to forget that Aristotle spent twenty years voluntarily in Plato's company.

When they split, the disagreement represented no physical danger to either. A bruised ego was the worst injury sustained. However, during the years with Plato, Aristotle did begin to acquire more menacing enemies. That perhaps didn't matter when he was at the Academy: any animosities were indulged through the medium of debate. However, when he left in 347 BCE, the year Plato died, his life started to look rather different. Personal risk became a real concern, and hence the need to be on the run. Coupled with the war-filled times in which he lived, two associations in particular were to cause him problems. One was his link with a tyrant called Hermias, the other was with Alexander the Great.

Hermias was the tyrant of Atarneus, a city on the coast of Asia Minor, in modern day Turkey. Aristotle travelled to Atarneus in 347 BCE because he had become one of the targets of the famous orator Demosthenes. Demosthenes had objected to the capture of a town north of Athens by the Macedonians. Aristotle had links with the Macedonian royal family as his father, Nicomachus, had been the doctor and friend of Amyntas III, the king of Macedon. Demosthenes' 'golden lips', as they were called, were more than capable of moving a crowd, and he moved them against Aristotle. Perhaps no longer benefiting from the protection of Plato, the philosopher decided he must leave Athens, and so sailed across the Aegean, and found Hermias.

Hermias was hospitable: being a tyrant didn't necessarily mean that he was a despot, for in ancient times, the term was used in a more technical way. An absolute ruler could be benign and good for his people. That Hermias was benevolent might have had something to do with the fact that he was also a friend of philosophy, having studied at Plato's Academy himself. Aristotle and he had met there. The overlapping webs of power and learning worked for Aristotle for a time. Hermias gave him and his disciples a place in a nearby city called Assos to live in, 'and they spent their time there in philosophy, meeting together in a courtyard, and Hermias provided them with all they needed'.

Aristotle stayed put for two or three years, and a deep relationship between himself and his patron was the result. The two sealed their friendship in bonds of kinship – Pythias, Aristotle's first wife, was Hermias' niece – though the popularity the alliance won him was subsequently to backfire.

It struck after Hermias' death. If he had been a good tyrant, he still had to climb the greasy pole to achieve his position, and some said he had done so by murdering a rival. The rumour stuck. He was betrayed by his enemies to the Persians, who tortured him to death. With Hermias' unfortunate departure,

Figure 12 Ruins of the Temple of Athena, Assos

Aristotle was again exposed. Once more, he had to up sticks. He returned to Stagira, his birthplace, and remained there until fortune appeared to turn in his favour once more.

That happened when he became tutor to the young Alexander, in 343 BCE. The lucrative appointment came about in part because of Aristotle's family connections at the Macedonian court. However, it was also the case that by the time a tutor for Alexander was being sought, Aristotle – now forty-one years of age – was established as Plato's most brilliant student, and a master in his own right. Philip sent out letters all around the Mediterranean, in the search for a teacher for his son, but in retrospect, there was only one serious candidate. Aristotle secured the post, and the remuneration. Another powerful relationship between two men of history was formed, Aristotle and Alexander: this time mental ferocity met military ambition.

It is fascinating to speculate on the encounter between the sage and the future conqueror. Bertrand Russell thought that a fiery Alexander would have been 'bored by the prosy old pedant'. Something of that pedantry rubbed off though. Aristotle carried out many scientific investigations during his life and developed a meticulous habit of gathering specimens and evidence. Alexander likewise came to ensure that biological specimens were collected wherever he and his armies travelled.

Mary Renault, the biographer of Alexander, thought differently to Russell. She believed that the relationship might have worked because Aristotle met Alexander's need for self-assurance. This was a vital quality to have if you would be king and ruler of half the world. Did Aristotle sense the energy that he was unleashing? Did he run the risk of trying to temper them? From what we know of Alexander, the task would have been as difficult as taming a lion.

One of the subjects he would have taught his mighty charge was politics. Aristotle was of the conviction that this subject was not an optional extra for humans. He believed that human beings are 'political animals'. It is in our nature to live in groups, which is to say that we have to live in groups in order to live at all. You could no more see an isolated human being living on planet Earth than you could a lonesome honey bee or a single ant. We, like they, are born for community, and if a moment should arrive in life when the human creature found him- or herself isolated and unpopular, he or she would be overcome by the natural desire to make new alliances and establish new friends. To be without company feels like a kind of death. So you can see that unpopularity was a serious business for Aristotle.

And it became a threat again as a result of educating the prince. Perhaps that is not surprising: he was inevitably to become embroiled in the ups and downs of real politics. One moment when that came to the fore was in 336 BCE. In the autumn of that year, King Philip, Alexander's father, met his end at the sharp end of an assassin's dagger. The murder took place in public, the murderer outwitting the guards. That led to much speculation that it was an inside job, perhaps performed with Alexander's blessing. After all, he was the main benefi-ciary of his father's death, and there was little love lost between them. Aristotle, though, disagreed – and risked the repercus-sions of putting his thoughts down on paper. He actually pro-vides us with the only contemporary note on what happened, and describes how the assassin had a personal vendetta against Philip. In other words, it had nothing to do with the relation-ships between members of the imperial family.

Aristotle's remark would have suited Alexander. He was allying himself with the king – and in real politics, to make one man your friend is to make another your enemy. There is no avoiding it. It is just the way of the world.

Politics is a game that can be played for the good of course, and Aristotle did on occasion manage to use his access to rulers well. On another occasion, during Alexander's reign in 330 BCE, Aristotle's popularity rating gained a boost. We know this because he was awarded an honour for services rendered in public life. The inscription survives: 'Let Aristotle and Callisthenes be praised and crowned and let the Stewards transcribe the table … and set it up in the temple.' Callisthenes was Aristotle's nephew. The inscription commemorates the research they undertook on the history of the Pythian Games. The honour was voted for the two in Delphi, home of the ancient Pythian oracle.

A sadder tale comes three years later. It again concerns Callisthenes. The now unlucky chap became implicated in a plot against Alexander's life, though he was probably guilty of nothing more than having a loose tongue. Alexander punished him by locking him in an iron cage. In it, Callisthenes literally rotted, aided by an infestation of vermin. He was finally thrown to a lion to end the torment. Aristotle must have mourned for his nephew, and worried no little for himself.

That there was good reason to do so finally became clear when Alexander died. This momentous event occurred in June 323 BCE and the dire ramifications for Aristotle quickly emerged. We know that within a few months he fled another adopted home, this time Athens again. The fortune he had previously enjoyed turned against him once more, and as before really through little fault of his own. What happened was this.

With Alexander gone, anti-Macedonianism was back in fashion in Athens. Worse, the anti-Macedonian party were democrats and they knew that Aristotle had ambivalent feelings about democracy. He feared rule by the people could descend into mob rule, and had written as much. These thoughts were easily, and perhaps deliberately, misrepresented. His newly empowered enemies took their chance in the power vacuum created by Alexander's death. This philosopher was Alexander's man, they whispered. He and his family were close to Athens' oppressors. Evidence that some wanted nothing less than Aristotle's blood comes – oddly enough – from the aforementioned inscription of 330, that recorded the honour awarded to Aristotle and Callisthenes. It only survives because it was found at the bottom of a well in Delphi. It had been hurled into the pit, presumably by a mob of democrats who had rallied and demonstrated against Aristotle.

As they smashed the plaque they may have insinuated that Aristotle had failed in his greatest duty: the education of Alexander. Why hadn't he tamed and tempered the man? Had he encouraged his expansionist ambitions? Surely this dandy had been wooed by wealth and power! A similar accusation had been made against Socrates. He had been the teacher of Alcibiades, another glamorous general who ended up fighting the Athenians. The association was not lost on Aristotle. He told friends that 'he did not want the Athenians to commit a second crime against philosophy', by being responsible for his death too.

In short, a lifetime of alliances had caught up with Aristotle. He had had to make them. For a man of the world, that was the only way to live. It bought him popularity for a time, and influence, which he tried to use well. But fortune had intervened conclusively with the death of Alexander. His luck had run out. He was now a man who was despised.

It must have been painful. Apart from everything else, he had founded and then run his school in Athens for thirteen years. Further, it was far from obvious that the institution would thrive in his absence, and it did in fact become less popular in the succeeding years, being eclipsed by the training-houses of other ancient philosophers such as the Epicureans and Stoics. Now, leaving it for the last time, Aristotle withdrew to an old family estate in Chalcis. Today, it is barely a couple of hours drive from Athens, plus a ferry ride. Then, it was a world away. Effectively in isolation and exile Aristotle did sometimes complain about being distant from events, though mostly he managed to find contentment. He wrote to one friend, Antipater: 'As for what was voted me at Delphi, of which I am now deprived, this is my attitude: I am neither greatly concerned by the matter, nor wholly unconcerned.'

So how did he deal with his unpopularity? Did a lifetime of philosophy help? It seems that it made all the difference.

Aristotle's will survives. Its details are touching. He remembers his daughter: 'if anything should happen to the girl (which heaven forbid and no such thing will happen) ...'. He entrusts the care of his younger children to Nicomachus, asking that he be 'both father and brother to them'. Herpyllis is well cared for too: 'she was very good to me,' Aristotle reflects, and he wants her to inherit a large proportion of his money and property. He asks that the bones of Pythias, his first wife, be buried alongside his. Aristotle also makes generous provision for his slaves: 'set them free as they deserve,' he instructs. And most strikingly for us, given the lonely condition of life he suffered at the last, the will opens with these words: 'All will be well.'

That strikes a positive note and conveys much about the temperament of the old man. He appears reconciled to the course of his life, though his luck had run out. He might well have concluded that he would die forgotten, the lyceum a failure. Bitterness was a risk. So what was the source of his good feeling?

Whilst in his early thirties, Aristotle had written an essay called 'Invitation to Philosophy' and it provides us with a clue.

The document doesn't survive in its entirety but what does indicates what he thought was the key to a lasting and durable contentment. He argues that reasoning and investigation are worth doing not because of what they might deliver – be that power or influence, wealth or popularity. Conversely, they should not be avoided for the ill-fortune they might bring. Rather, philosophy and science are good for their own sake. They train their adherents in the contemplation of life, the understanding of the universe, the value of being human. Aristotle approves of what an earlier philosopher, Anaxagoras, had said when he asked himself what was the meaning of life: 'To observe the heavens, and the stars and moon and sun in them.' Aristotle believed that it was for this purpose that human beings had been made, it was this goal that made sense of their godlike intellect. And such a quality, properly cultivated, can ride the storms of any misfortune, even the unpopularity that can be so damaging to the wellbeing of human creatures, the 'political animal'.

In another place, his *Ethics*, Aristotle said something similar, and it reads like a gloss on the phrase with which he opened his will:

> We must not heed those who advise us to think as human beings since we are human and to think mortal things since we are mortal, but we must be like immortals insofar as possible and do everything toward living in accordance with the best thing in us.

Aristotle felt he had realised the best thing in him, his powers of reason. He was unpopular but could die with equanimity. After all that had happened to him, he could still assert that all will be well. If you can say that of yourself, the opinion of others will not matter. Such is the advice he would offer us.

CHAPTER 7

Pyrrho of Elis on suspending disbelief

It might be said that we live in a world that above all else longs to *know*. When we take a train, we expect to know the departure and arrival times to the nearest minute. When we become ill, we expect the doctor to know the prognosis, and to tell it to us straight. When we save some money, we demand guarantees on the rates of return, and take out insurance policies to mitigate against any losses. Similarly, there are people now who would sue a teacher who confessed a gap in their knowledge, and crucify a politician who admitted to making an error. The current obsession with certainty would have astonished our forbears only a generation or two ago.

It's at least partly because of science. Science is by far and away the most successful means humanity has invented for the delivery of knowledge. With it comes a culture that celebrates laws, solutions, measurements and truths. It is one that prefers sunlight to starlight, clarity to mystery, evidence to ideas. It is this culture that holds so much sway today.

But is something lost in such a black and white world? Instead of deciding whether something is believable or not – true or not – could there be a gain in suspending disbelief, holding off on deciding, being open to the possibility that we do not and may not ever know? Keats called it the Negative Capability, 'being in uncertainties, mysteries, doubts without any irritable reaching after fact and reason'. Coleridge before him celebrated the 'suspended state', and thought this was the source of any real imagination.

Ancient philosophy emerged during a period in which science was first gaining a grip on the imagination. It produced a first generation of tremendous theories, such as that the world might be made of matter, and technological feats, such as the building of the Parthenon in Athens. Individuals such as Aristotle came next. However, there were philosophers who worried that things were getting out of balance. They may act as guides if our world too has become unbalanced by the lust for certainty.

Pyrrho of Elis is a good case in point. He was born around 365 BCE in the north west Peloponnese, and was philosophically minded from an early age. I imagine him as an art student, exposed to radical ideas in his youth, and encouraged to experiment by putting them into practice. 'Life imitates Art far more than Art imitates Life,' wrote Oscar Wilde in his essay *The Decay of Lying*. Pyrrho might have adhered to that.

He fell under the sway first of Stilpo of Megara and then of Anaxarchus of Abdera. Both of these philosophers were known for their indifference to things, as captured in dramatic stories. Stilpo was said to have let marauders pillage his house without once protesting; his wisdom was his only valuable possession, he said, and they couldn't take that. Anaxarchus, also known as 'the contented', was condemned to death by a jealous Cypriot tyrant, his execution to be carried out by pounding in a large mortar. He replied that it was the mortar that would be pounded, not Anaxarchus.

Anaxarchus also travelled to India, following the armies of Alexander the Great. Pyrrho, now aged about thirty-five, went with him and the trip became a turning point in his life. As a young man, he had desired fame and desperately sought the approval of others, a lust for recognition that inculcated a restless spirit and impetuous temper – the art student who seeks assurance that he or she has made a mark on the world. However, in India, Pyrrho seems to have had something of a conversion experience, or at least the place enabled him to see how his desires would ruin him if they were not wisely channelled.

He stayed there for about eighteen months, for some of that time in Taxila, in modern day Pakistan, close to the Murree hills and alongside the Tamra-Nala river. This is where the famous 'naked philosophers' lived, the Gymnosophists, so-called because they happily went about unclothed. One day he heard one of them reproaching his master, Anaxarchus, for teaching about the good life whilst doing little to nurture the good in himself. 'You will never be able to teach others what is good while you dance attendance on kings in their courts,' the sage jibed. It struck a cord with Pyrrho. Fawning on someone in an obsequious manner was just what he was liable to do. From then on, he realised that he must put his efforts into the *practice* of his philosophy, rather than its articulation or expression. He determined to give up his childish ways and learn seriousness and serenity.

During the next period of his life he developed a number of techniques aimed at reorientating his youthful drives. Perhaps the most obvious was temporarily to retire from the business of the world, find a retreat and spend time in solitude. He adopted a mantra too, a line from Homer: 'As leaves on trees, such is the life of man.' He recited it repeatedly, like a prayer:

there's a tip for recovering some balance when it comes to security and certainty.

He also learnt to value discussion with whomever he found himself, high-and-mighty and common-or-garden. He no longer looked down on anyone and, moreover, felt unperturbed when the listeners he did have took no notice and drifted off, leaving him standing alone. He would calmly finish what he had to say and move on.

Back in Greece, he went to live with his sister, and was not ashamed to do women's work – dusting in the house, taking pigs and poultry to market. He had found sangfroid. There is a story that once whilst travelling by sea, he remained content during a storm of such ferocity that it unnerved all the other passengers.

Pyrrho also found an ability to laugh at himself. One day, he was spotted falling back in fright when a vicious dog attacked

Figure 13 *The philosopher Pyrrho on a stormy sea* by Petrarca-Meister, Pyrrho seated with equanimity against the central mast

him. A passer-by, and critic, thought he had caught the immovable one out. Pyrrho, composure regained, chuckled. 'It is not easy always to be calm,' he admitted. 'We must work at practising what we preach.'

It was this disposition that he exhibited in his maturity which won him many followers. In later years, his home town made him a high priest, which is remarkable given that some of his peers must have remembered him as the arty, arrogant child; a prophet is not usually welcome in his own town. Timon of Phlius was one such witness. Whilst he dismissed most of the philosophers of the time as wafflers or windbags, he detected something original and authentic in Pyrrho:

> This, O Pyrrho, my heart yearns to hear, how on earth you, though a man, act most easily and calmly, never taking thought and consistently undisturbed, heedless of the whirling motions and sweet voices of wisdom? You alone led the way for men, like the god who drives around the whole earth as he revolves, showing the blazing disk of his well-rounded sphere.

Pyrrho was like Socrates in that he wrote nothing. He had thoroughly internalised the lesson of the Indian yogis: practice is all, personal example is more powerful than words. He did not want his followers to quibble over his reflections but to follow his pattern of life. That said, he was repeatedly asked questions and implored to expound his point of view – no doubt by youths who were as in need of surety about themselves as he had been. Sometimes, the demands were too much: one day, pressed in between a crowd and a river, he stripped and swam to the other bank to escape.

There is another, more subtle, reason he resisted giving sermons. It is not just the practice that counts but the journey that is made. Only by staying the course can the individual embody the truth, as opposed to learning merely to spout it. Doctrine tends to be static. Such formulas come at the end of the deliberation, they are the culmination of a search, and if people just repeat the formulas they may never suffer the deliberation, the experience of uncertainty that is actually so valuable. For above all, Pyrrho wanted them to learn one thing: how to suspend disbelief, to be happy not to know, to nurture that negative capability. This was the attitude and spirit that underlay his mature belief.

We can explore more of what that might mean by examining some of his sayings. A handful of them survive and they are fascinating to ponder. To take them seriously, you are forced to peer through what they appear to be saying on the surface, and penetrate to what they might more deeply imply, which is to say to be prepared at the outset not merely to ask whether they are simply true or false. Here's one:

Nothing really exists, but human life is governed by convention.

This is ostensibly an hyperbolic statement. It seemingly implies that the world of experience and facts is a delusion and that all that we do and think is a kind of agreement or pact, not true in itself.

Consider this statement too:

Nothing is in itself more this than that.

Aristotle, Pyrrho's near contemporary and a man who disagreed with him as a pioneer of science, tackled this piece of logic and declared it uroboric, that is, it devours itself like the Ouroboros serpent that eats its own tail. If an affirmation is no more true than its negation, then there is no way of discerning the difference between the affirmation and the negation. Aristotle would have declared Pyrrho's thoughts nonsensical, and so unworthy of any place in the kingdom of expanding human knowledge.

But Aristotle misunderstood. These statements were not supposed to be taken at face value. Rather, they were supposed, like a koan, to jolt you into perceiving something deeper about reality precisely as a result of their apparent contradiction. If you could rest for a moment in apparent ignorance, then a more imaginative and subtle insight might be the result. Perhaps the closest we can get to this method today is by comparison with Buddhist beliefs. (The two were probably close in origin, given the Greeks' exploration of India.)

The first, 'Nothing really exists, but human life is governed by convention', is like the Buddhist idea that everything is caused by something else. Everything is related to something or other; there is no unconditioned ground upon which to stand. It is not just that all effects have causes, but all causes have causes too. This can cause confusion. It is existentially unsettling, like suddenly realising you are treading water over unfathomable depths. You look down and there is no bottom. But peer again into that flux, Pyrrho suggests, and convert any fear about its impenetrability into a curiosity about its density. Such is the nature of your consciousness, your personality, your experience. The net result is that anxiety dissolves as your interest rises. 'Nothing really exists' becomes an invitation not a curse.

The second surviving fragment, 'Nothing is in itself more this than that', can be taken as being close to the Buddhist notion of giving up on craving or grasping at things. When you realise that nothing is in itself more this than that, it is possible to sit more easily with this and that, or whatever life throws at you. Tumult gives way to tranquillity.

Such insights cannot really be learnt, though; you have to find your way into them, they are more seen than explained. Hence the emphasis in Pyrrhonism on practice. The way to do that is to defer how you presume the world to be, and explore how it might be otherwise. It is a willing suspension of disbelief.

The approach is captured in the original meaning of the word 'sceptic'. It implied something different from what it does today. Rather than someone who is disbelieving or incredulous it meant someone who was a seeker or inquirer. So to be a sceptic was to be in pursuit of a perception that you have as yet not wholly realised, or only glimpsed on occasion. Contradictions are in this way useful; in their assertions, and then their undermining of the assertion, they keep the sceptic questing. To deploy the technical term, Scepticism is a dialectical way of life. In Buddhist terms, what is sought is the Middle Way – the Middle Way that is excluded if, like Aristotle, you insist on a purely logical analysis of statements and doctrines as a means to knowledge. Pyrrho was offering an alternative way of life, one in which investigation was carried out not so much by scientific means but by intuitive ones. Pyrrhonists insisted that their statements were not positive convictions but were rather negative guides – negative in the sense of working to negate appearances. They didn't draw conclusions but made more comparisons. They didn't pass rational judgement but continued with the imaginative examination.

In life, a completely sceptical attitude is hard to sustain. It is more likely that individuals will fluctuate between periods when they successfully suspend their convictions and peer more deeply into things, and periods when they rest on the more or less certain intuitions of the humdrum. Many such beliefs will be those that are simply necessary to get through the day: suddenly to take 'nothing exists' at face value would mean you'd never get up in the morning. Science – with its laws and solutions, facts and reasons – has its uses, not least if you want to take a train, find out that you are ill and don't want to lose all your money. But what the Sceptics sensed was that however concrete your immediate experience of the world might appear, a moment's reflection reveals a less robust constitution for things, and a lifetime's reflection delivers the insight that nothing can be said to exist in its essence.

What can be made of this way of life today, especially if you are not a Buddhist? Some hold Scepticism as a doctrine, often calling it relativism. Relativism is the belief that nothing is true – though, of course, if nothing is true, then relativism itself isn't either. As a doctrine, then, relativism consumes its tail the minute it opens its mouth. That reveals the fundamental mistake of embracing Scepticism as if it were a system of metaphysics, though such is the lust for certainty in life that people prefer the consolation of assertions such as 'nothing exists', to giving up on assertions *tout à fait*. No, Pyrrho says. The true Sceptic has got to live the life.

Perhaps it is possible to identify some more recent examples of when this has been achieved, at least to a degree. A case in point might be the private reflections of Charles Darwin. When he was writing the *Origin of Species* he often felt a strong conviction about the existence of God. What he sensed is 'the extreme difficulty or rather impossibility of conceiving of this immense and wonderful universe, including man with his capability of looking far backwards and far into futurity, as the result of blind chance or necessity'. He felt compelled to postulate a first cause, with an intelligent mind, that lay behind creation. However, as he thought on, this conviction grew weaker. And it was a Pyrrhonian attitude of doubt, as opposed to a scientific proof, that caused this diminution. 'Can the mind of man, which has, as I fully believe, been developed from a mind as low as that possessed by the lowest animal, be trusted when it draws such grand conclusions?' Darwin saw into the mind of human beings, and noted a tendency to draw grand conclusions that really lacked any basis, given the immense unknowns that surround us. His agnosticism was a kind of sceptical awakening.

Another reflection of contemporary Scepticism might take a lead from the report that Pyrrho was originally a painter. Given that is true, it is perhaps not surprising to find a pretty consistent example of lived Pyrrhonism in the life of the British sculptor, Henry Moore.

Moore's suspension of judgement, in relation to his work, came out in an interview in which he described being sent a book about his art by a Jungian theorist, and being asked to

Figure 14 *Two Piece Reclining Figure No. 5* by Henry Moore, bronze, sited in the grounds of Kenwood House, London (Photo: Andrew Dunn)

read it. The book purported to understand and explain his work, to decipher its truth. Moore hesitated when he had the book in his hands. He explained why:

After the first chapter I thought I'd better stop because it explained too much about what my motives were. I thought it might stop me from ticking over if I went on and knew it all. I prefer really to not talk about one's work too much, not to try to explain it too much. One can say things that don't matter, yes. But to try to go into its deep motives and reasons I think stops – might stop – one from wanting to go on.

What is fascinating about these comments is that Moore sensed the book might offer a partial explanation, within its own terms of reference. And yet he knew that really there is no complete explanation of his work to be had, and certainly no explanation that could surpass what the work itself could show. So he preferred not to be encumbered by the knowledge, not to reach out after fact and reason, to recall Keats' phrase, and instead keep pursuing his imaginative obsession with the female and maternal form.

The risk of the explanation is that in its apparent fullness it might claim and exclude the unknown forces that drove him. It's not that there is nothing that could be said about him or his work. Rather it is knowing when to stop that is key, knowing when a theory, in its demand to understand all, might actually quench the animating spirit.

Moore also talked about how striving for a perfection you know you can't reach is much more valuable than achieving a perfection that is easy. Again, this is an aspect that the Sceptic understands – that which lies beyond telling.

Another great creative figure of modern times was the

founder of psychoanalysis, Sigmund Freud. In his biography of the man, *The Death of Sigmund Freud*, Mark Edmundson sums up the attitude towards life and its big questions that he felt Freud had attained at the end. It can act as a conclusion for us here, as it reads as a kind of Pyrrhonist's *credo* – as in a way of life, not a set of doctrines:

> To Freud, the self-aware person [the Sceptic] is continually in the process of deconstructing various god replacements and returning once again to a more sceptical and ironic middle ground. The sane, or relatively sane, self is constantly being duped by this Truth or that (the hunger is very strong; that's simply the way we are) and then coming back to himself and finding more reasonable authorities. He's perpetually consulting his experience, sifting data, questing amid the knowledge of the past and the day-to-day life of the present to find out what is good in the way of belief. He'll ultimately surrender neither to the belief in nothing, nor to the belief in the great One. His life is one of constant self-criticism, and even then he's perpetually surprised at how often he falls for another idol or decides, however wittingly, to give it up and to believe he believes nothing. But his is also a life of discovery and pleasure at the unexpected, if provisional, truths and fresh possibilities that the world throws his way. He feels, on balance, more than fortunate to be alive.

CHAPTER 8

Epicurus on why
less is more

You have to feel sorry for Epicurus. Of all the ancient philosophers, he is arguably the most misunderstood. His very name has become a byword for exactly the opposite of what he stood for: an epicurean, according to my dictionary, is someone who is devoted to sensual pleasures. That conjures up images of excessive hedonism, indulgent gratification, decadent desire.

In fact, his life manifested an extraordinary commitment to a philosophy that could be one for our consumer age too. It can be summed up in three, short words: less is more.

He was born in 342 BCE, on the island of Samos, close to Asia Minor, an Athenian colony at the time. At the age of eighteen, he travelled to Athens, and then did not return to his home. The intervening death of Alexander the Great sent waves of political unrest and disturbance around the Mediterranean basin, and Samos was no longer safe. He went instead to Colophon, on the Asia Minor mainland. Colophon was a beautiful place. In Greek the word means 'summit', and the city was the crowning glory of a ridge of hills. What was particularly attractive to

Epicurus was that it was near another town called Teos, and there lived a philosopher called Nausiphanes.

Nausiphanes had been taught by Pyrrho, and he was also an aficionado of the natural philosophy of Democritus of Abdera. A century or so before Epicurus, this man had travelled widely through the Middle East and as far as India. He lived to be over 100 years old. He had developed the theory of atoms that Epicurus was to adopt too. In fact, it became the fundamental grounding for his way of life.

You might say that the atomic model of things is about as simple an hypothesis as you could imagine. All the subtlety and complexity of the universe boils down to these fundamental, indivisible units of stuff, out of which everything else is made. It is an understanding of physics that strips away all excessive speculation and arrives at a conjecture built upon a minimal number of elegant basics. From that simplicity, everything else follows. You can see how it would have appealed to Epicurus. It suggested that his principle, less is more, was written into the fabric of the cosmos.

Epicurus could not see atoms, of course, any more than Democritus could. Rather, he reasoned that they must exist. If matter were *infinitely* divisible then in theory you would be able to divide and divide and divide until you were left with nothing. But, of course, something cannot come out of nothing. Therefore, matter cannot be infinitely divisible. It must consist of indivisible units, which were called atoms.

These atoms, the theory continued, occupy a void, and are always moving. They combine after colliding to form compounds, and it is from these compounds that the objects and bodies we see in the world are formed. How we see the objects and bodies around us – their colours, smells, sounds – has to do with how we perceive the atoms, as opposed to how they are in themselves. Then again, our perceptions are but the result of the rearrangement of atoms in our own bodies, for we are nothing but atoms too. As Democritus put it: 'By convention sweet, by convention bitter, by convention hot, by convention cold, but in reality atoms and void.'

This world of bits speeding aimlessly through eternal emptiness might seem a cold universe to postulate. To the Epicureans, though, it was a liberation. We are material beings living in a material world with nothing except matter to worry about. In other words, we are already entirely at home.

That said, not many accepted these teachings. Atoms were a neat idea. It just seemed that they were too reductive an idea as well. How does the experience of colour result from the rearrangement of particulate specks? How can randomly whizzing iotas amount to the moral qualities of human experience, such as beauty, goodness and free will? We don't see these atoms, or have the vaguest intimations of their existence, so where's the evidence?

Most Greeks regarded atomism as eccentric. Epicurus, though, didn't. There was perhaps a personal as well as philosophical appeal in it for him since its minimalism fitted with his rather austere character, one that seems to have been quite puritanical. Either as a result, or as a cause, he had poor health. One of his disciples, Metrodorus, wrote a whole book about it, entitled *On the Weak Constitution of Epicurus*. Not that there is any point in worrying about illness, Epicurus thought. It's just the working out of the atoms. Indeed, pleasure itself is mostly the absence of pain, and pain shouldn't be taken that seriously, either. Aches, hurts, sores and torments are only atomic collisions, if unfortunate ones. When he died in 270 BCE, of excruciatingly painful kidney stones, Epicurus didn't complain once. His final letter to another friend, Hermarchus, recorded his feelings:

On the happiest, and the last, day of my life. I am suffering from diseases of the bladder and intestines, which are of the utmost possible severity. Yet all my sufferings are counterbalanced by the contentment of soul which I derive from remembering our reasonings and discoveries.

If you accept the testimony of that letter, then it must have been the case that Epicurus embodied the philosophy that less is more in a quite extraordinary way. As atomism stripped away the complexity of the universe to perceive the basic units of nature, so he was able to see through the complications of his agonising condition – how it affected him emotionally and mentally as well as physically – and accept it for what it was. Just illness.

Perhaps the Epicurean therapy worked like this. If you can believe in materialism, really believe it, then you can cut loose

Figure 15 Bust of Epicurus, from the Louvre, Paris

from many of the burdens that occupy others. There is no need to worry about the gods, for they have no control over the movement of the atoms. There is no need to fear death, for it is just a cessation of the movement of atoms. There is no need to be anxious about pain, as we have just seen. There is also no need to read portents, as the superstitious ancients were wont to do. A tree might be struck by lightning. The gods might seem to demand the sacrifice of a ram or cock. Someone would receive a 'vision'. An old myth might warn you off wandering through a sacred grove. Dump these tales, ignore the 'signs', Epicurus recommended. As atoms move under their own steam through the void, so the gods leave humankind to work out their own happiness, to shape their own future. Lightning and visions alike are nothing but the effects of streams of particles. The gods are no more likely to see you making that sacrifice than they are to appear to you in the grove. 'Moreover, when it comes to meteorological phenomena, one must believe that movements, turnings, eclipses, risings, settings, and related phenomena occur without any god helping out and ordaining or being about to ordain things,' he continued. Epicureanism explains them all, and explains them all away.

It sounds very modern. And when you take the philosophy seriously, when you don't just believe it but it seeps into the interstices of your existence, something remarkable happens. The scripts that so many live by, break up. The constraints that hold others back, dissolve. The very happiness of the gods becomes possible to realise in this life. The source of their bliss, Epicurus thought, was living according to their nature. If you accept atomism as the fundamental truth of your mortal nature, then you can enjoy divine-like happiness too.

At the most basic it helps us to appreciate our limitations – another reflection on the principle that less is more. Think about the desire to be happy, for example. When people say they want to be happy, they tend not to mean just that they want to be happy now, but that they want to be happy indefinitely into the future, more and more and more to enjoy happiness. But this longitudinal hope is difficult to guarantee, not least because sooner or later we will die. And this causes something else, a sense of foreboding, which can then itself become a cause of unhappiness, or at least less happiness.

How can Epicurus mitigate the paradox that the desire for happiness actually breeds unhappiness? He notes that any happiness you have now is already inherently limited, since in any single instant there is only so much pleasure you can enjoy anyway. That will be the same for all the subsequent moments of happiness you might have in the future. So, if you consider the nature of time, and regard it as a series of limited instances, you will quickly appreciate that happiness itself is inherently limited too, regardless of how long you live. 'Unlimited time and limited time contain equal amounts of pleasure, if one measures its limits by reasoning,' he surmises. The lesson, then, is that happiness is limited, period – regardless of its longevity. Accept that, and you might be a lot happier; accept his principle, less is more, and limitations themselves can become a blessing.

Pursuing that point further, Epicurus would have us ask just what the fundamental needs of life are, and what are redundant extras. He did just that and concluded that there are three types of thing that people say they need – and in fact they need only one of them. So, if you can be rid of the two that are redundant, you will live both more modestly – well within the inherent limitations of life – and more contentedly. Here's the relevant maxim: 'Of desires, some are natural and necessary, some natural and unnecessary, and some neither natural nor necessary but occurring as a result of groundless opinion.' So again what did he mean?

Take first an example of a natural and necessary desire, namely for water. Everyone needs water to quench their thirst and live. So, it is wise to want water, and water can make you very happy. That, then, is an example of a natural and necessary need.

However, an unnecessary need could follow from it, and so provide us with an example of the second category (and the first to jettison) of a natural but unnecessary need. The case in point might be *bottled* water. Everyone needs water to quench their thirst and live. However, someone who does not have the benefit of Epicurean philosophy might take that natural need and develop it into an obsession about the 'need' for bottled water. They might tell themselves that tap water can't be trusted, it doesn't taste as good or that they feel cheap when they ask for 'tap' in a restaurant. But in so doing they are compounding their needs unnecessarily. That way unhappiness lies. It is a manifestation of the erroneous philosophy that more is more. So, Epicurus would advise declining the option of bottled water.

In fact, bottled water is also an example of the third, unnatural and unnecessary need too. For what is unnatural about bottled water, as well as unnecessary, is that it is so expensive. That much seems obvious when forking out bank notes for the stuff, as you can in some restaurants. But even a cheap bottle of water is unnaturally dear. For example, one that costs only £1 is already about three times as expensive by volume as the petrol you put in your car. That water, which falls out of the sky, should be vastly dearer than oil, which costs a fortune to leach from the ground, is what makes expensive bottled water both unnatural and unnecessary – and so deeply implicated in an unepicurean way of life.

Epicurus' influence grew. He set up a school near the Academy of Plato, and called it the Garden. What was learnt there was to last for centuries. Perhaps it found its greatest flowering in the pen of the poet Lucretius. 'On the Nature of Things' is a classic of world literature. Here he writes about atoms:

> For since they wander through the void inane,
> All the primordial germs of things must needs
> Be borne along, either by weight their own,
> Or haply by another's blow without.
> For, when, in their incessancy so oft
> They meet and clash, it comes to pass again
> They leap asunder, face to face: not strange –
> Being most hard, and solid in their weights,
> And naught opposing motion, from behind.
> And that more clearly thou perceive how all
> These mites of matter are darted round about,
> Recall to mind how nowhere in the sum
> Of All exists a bottom, – nowhere is
> A realm of rest for primal bodies; since
> (As amply shown and proved by reason sure)
> Space has no bound nor measure, and extends
> Unmetered forth in all directions round.

Epicureanism was a clever philosophy not just for its content but for its form too. It could be embraced at many different levels. For example, you might just want to adopt a motto such as 'Death is nothing' or 'Don't fear the gods'. Many did, if the Greek and Roman rings and mirrors that have been found with those words etched on them are anything to go by. Next, you could pursue the implications of that possibility in other parts of your life, or seek to become more deeply persuaded of it:

Epicurus wrote letters for your perusal. The ones that survive read almost like self-help manuals, and freely circulated in the ancient world. Or you could push more deeply into it again. It is said that his main treatise on natural philosophy – his discussion of stuff like the atoms – amounted to a total of thirty-seven volumes. There was plenty to sink your teeth into.

But the message itself always remained short, for the message was itself the virtue of less, not more. Focus on the few natural and necessary needs in life and you will find that you live a lot more easily.

CHAPTER 9

Zeno of Citium on the psychology of shopping

In times of economic adjustment, people make adjustments too. Sometimes they may become convinced that less is more, and act on that new conviction. But often not. Rather – and for example – it is reportedly the case that, in times of economic hardship, sales of basic items for home cooking actually go up: we stock up on everything from butter to bouillon as we decide to spoil ourselves at home, rather than in a restaurant. Alternatively, people shop more precisely from lists, as opposed to reaching willy-nilly for goods from the shelves; they remember that the goal of shopping is to feed themselves not the bin, but they still keep buying. If you throw fears about damaging the environment into the mix, then habits shift gear again, and once more in illuminating ways. Consider this: research shows that we buy fewer bath products but more shower products when thinking about the planet. It would seem that ditching the elemental pleasures of a good soak altogether is too much to ask, though we are prepared to recognise that a shower is greener.

In summary, we react to times of boom and times of bust by making personal re-evaluations. And one of the key places those re-evaluations tangibly manifest themselves is in the items that we buy and devour. This must be what it means to be that modern creation, a consumer.

Turn it around then, and behaviour in the shops can be thought of as a key indicator of personality. What passes under the scanner at the check-out is far more than just a comment on your needs. It yields clues as to your character, your contentment, your longings. Someone who stocks up with chocolate on a Monday could be facing an unhappy week at work. Someone who religiously buys roses every Friday – a habit that the database shows he's had for the last ten years – might one day have to face up to the fact that he is in a loveless marriage that roses cannot save. Another person, who in the winter months piles the trolley high with strawberries imported from the other side of the world, might save herself the pennies, and the planet the carbon, if she moved to a place in the sun.

All this is why supermarkets are so keen to know the exact details of what you buy, and when. The data turns marketing into a much more precise science. And it might also explain why one ancient philosopher in particular became especially associated with shops. For him, retail outlets were excellent places to do philosophy because retail outlets are where you practise – wittingly or not – your philosophy of life.

In fact, the ancient Mediterranean was nothing if not a thoroughfare for merchants, and mercantilism was the lifeblood of the ancient Greek world. Trading by sea was the activity that made Athens great. Greek settlements and cities sprang up at virtually all habitable sites along the vast, oval coastline. Plato described them as like frogs around a pond. But the Mediterranean was also a life-taker. It frequently turned against seafarers in deadly squalls and sudden storms. The waters around the islands that littered the journey between, say, Cyprus and Piraeus, Athens' port, were treacherous, scattering the passage with many nautical traps.

Pirates were another hazard; in ancient Greek times the sea was the haunt of bandits. And there was the tendency to overload ships, to squeeze in another consignment. One more marble column or another dozen amphoras of oil could make the difference between a profit and a loss in what was always a marginal business – though the extra weight might additionally cause the vessel to become unstable.

Scholars today reckon that up to one in twenty ships that traversed the waters of the eastern Mediterranean sank. Over one thousand shipwrecks from before 1500 have been discovered to date. Their cargos and many, many members of their crews would not have reached their destinations. They would have drifted slowly to the muddy bottom of the blue ocean.

Zeno of Citium's father, Mnaseas, was one of the traders who took these risks. He was a merchant and made a fortune from porphyry, the purple rock that the Egyptians, the Greeks and then the Romans associated with imperial might and royalty. Citium, where the family came from, is a port on Cyprus' eastern shore. Mnaseas exchanged these goods in Athens, for although by the end of the fourth century when Zeno was born, its glory was beginning to fade, it was still an important city. It would remain a centre of culture and knowledge for centuries.

It was perhaps for this reason that Zeno anxiously awaited the return of his father. From his earliest days, the gangly, swarthy child – whose nickname was 'vine-branch' – had shown a precocious interest in learning. Mnaseas had taken to buying his son reading material from the booksellers of the Athenian marketplace. All sorts of texts would have made their way into Zeno's home; tragedies, comedies, poems and dialogues. And occasionally amongst the scrolls was a copy of what were to become the young scholar's prized possessions, works written by the now long-dead Plato.

Plato's dialogues, as invitations to philosophy, would have been as enticing to a youth with an enquiring spirit as, say, Philip Pullman's *His Dark Materials* trilogy or C.S. Lewis' *Chronicles of Narnia* are to a child with the capacity to wonder. Their joy is that they want you to participate in philosophy, because philosophy only lives when it leaps off the page.

It did leap for Zeno. He dreamt of travelling to Athens. Plato was gone. Philosophy was not, and as it would turn out, it would live on in no small part due to Zeno himself. He was to found his own philosophy school, of equal influence to that of Plato.

First he had to get to Athens. That was more difficult than it might seem. Although his kindly father had fed his son's interests, there were the family interests to take care of first. In due course, when he succeeded Mnaseas as the head of the firm, Zeno conducted trips around the Mediterranean, though with strict instructions to trade porphyry, not philosophy. So his chance did not come until he was about the age of thirty.

What happened was this. On one journey, his ship was struck by one of the many Mediterranean hazards. Zeno was shipwrecked, though as luck would have it, just off-land from Piraeus. We do not know what happened to his cargo or crew, only that Zeno made it into the city. From now on, a new course was set. 'It is well done of thee, Fortune, thus to drive me to philosophy,' he later declared. He headed straight for a bookseller.

There, he picked up a copy of Xenophon's *Memorabilia*, a memoir of Socrates written by another of his first followers. Zeno turned to Book Two, where Xenophon records a number of conversations the sage was supposed to have had, as well as stories about him. The section opens with a notion that was to become central to Zeno's own way of life. Socrates is discussing how a child should be educated. He makes the observation that although people are taught many things in school, it is often the most basic skills that are overlooked, skills such as how to get a good night's sleep or how to contain the frustration of not being able to find the items they want in the shops. Training in these matters would be enormously useful, Socrates observes. Zeno agreed.

Stoicism – as the tradition to which Zeno gave rise is called – is a full philosophy. It ranges over ideas about the physics of the universe and the logic of human thought. Zeno himself ended up writing dozens of works including some inspired by those of Plato, like *Republic*, and others with titles such as *Of Emotions*, *Of Duty*, *Of Law*, *Of Signs* – though none survive. However, his ideas about ethics are perhaps what inspired his followers the most. They came to value his stoical attitude to life. Though we have a different understanding of the word today.

Figure 16 Zeno, bearded as a philosopher (Cast in Pushkin Museum from original in Naples)

A fundamental concept in Zeno's thinking is self-preservation. Animals and humans alike have a basic propensity to choose those options that make life better for them, and avoid those actions that are dangerous. It sounds selfish. It is. And yet, Zeno's point is not to affirm selfishness per se. It is more to recognise that selfishness is an irredeemable element within the psyche of any living creature.

However, not all living creatures are the same. For most animals, the good will consist in things like finding food, shelter, a mate. For humans, who do not just survive but also think, another element comes into play, namely the exercise of our capacity to do good, to be good, to think well. We must take care of our souls as well as our bodies. If eating and copulating are the therapies of desire, insight and philosophy are the therapies of thought.

This higher element, that is the determining characteristic of the human animal, at least as the Stoics had it, profoundly modifies our relationship to our innate selfishness. Zeno and his followers conjured up extreme examples to illustrate what they meant. If, say, I am being tortured by a tyrant to confess to something that is not the truth, it will be in my higher interests to suffer the torment and keep quiet. I may even choose to die rather than lie. That hardly contributes to my preservation as an animal. It does, though, as a human being; it preserves my integrity, reason and thought. Moreover, to suffer the agony and risk my life for the sake of the truth would be, in a sense, to sacrifice myself. Such courage could therefore be called a kind of selflessness. Paradoxically, human selfishness can be selfless.

In this way, Stoics averred, you could be happy whilst in torment on the ancient Greek equivalent of the rack, because you could know you were preserving the best that was in you. An animal could never feel that, or at least so we presume. In a similar vein, Stoics also believed that committing suicide can sometimes be the best course of action, and several Stoics were remembered for doing so. Cleanthes starved himself. Seneca bled himself. Cicero held out his head to meet the sword. Zeno himself died by holding his breath – a feat that medical science says is impossible, though it demonstrated to Zeno's followers how totally he had mastered the way of life he commended.

The stoical attitude towards suffering and suicide was one result of Zeno's new interpretation of Socrates' teaching that it is not just living that counts for humans, but living well. A decent training in that would be a training that makes for a better life. And it takes training, as being able to withstand torture and face your own death implies.

Stoicism is not just about being able to grin and bear it though. There is a positive side to this way of life, focused on the cultivation of virtue. Virtues – such as the courage and fortitude required to be stoical, though including others such as prudence and justice – are important because they are the qualities of life that are manifest in a vibrant soul: they bring out the good in us and make for our wellbeing. Other elements in life, like having wealth or health, are inconsequential, above a minimum level, when compared to this most important part.

Incidentally, this meant you could be a Stoic if you were rich as well as poor, if you were vigorous in body or afflicted by disease. That universality of application was no small part of Stoicism's widespread appeal, though the wealthy had to be careful: Zeno also taught that a preoccupation with riches or health can be dangerous, easily distracting an individual from the narrow path that leads to the virtues which matter.

If that much sounds fairly obvious, Zenonians derived other genuinely penetrating insights. One concerned the judgements you make in response to events. Zeno imagined breaking them down according to their strengths. Consider travelling on board a ship. A squall blows up, and the sailor sees a wave rushing towards him. Analysing the situation simply, he can be thought of as making one judgement when he acknowledges the danger and perhaps tries to act to reduce the impact of the wave. But he may also experience a more excessive judgement if, seeing the danger, he is overwhelmed with the fear of what it could do to him. The risk is that the latter experience over-whelms the former and incapacitates the sailor. He will then be much more likely to die. That, though, should not happen to the well-trained Stoic, whose responses will be proportionate and measured.

The way to develop such an ability, and so act for your own good, is to practise the anticipation of bad things. Try this. At the beginning of the day, rehearse in your mind every bad thing that could happen to you during the day – from losing your job, to being run over by a bus, to being dumped by your partner. If you do practise this pessimism, quite thoroughly and seriously, the Stoic contention is that you will be more pre-pared to live the day well, according to your higher nature, and in turn, live more happily too. At dawn, distress. During the day, delight.

Epictetus, the Roman Stoic, was one of Zeno's followers who developed a related practice. Imagine waking up, he muses in his handbook for good living, and immediately becoming anx-ious about thoughts, say, on whether you should punish your slave lest he become lax, or cut him some slack since his life is hard. That is an unfortunate way to start the day, Epictetus thought, for two reasons.

First, it means that you are subject to uncontrolled mental perturbations; note how long the anxiety about your slave persists, the energy and momentum it gains as you worry. If your day starts like this, it is hardly likely to get better.

Second, your slave is supposed to make life easier for you, and yet he is making it harder! So, Epictetus advises, actively consider that your slave may not come when he is called, and even if he does come, he may not do what you bid. And then, let that concern go. 'It is better that your servant should be bad than you unhappy.'

Epictetus continues: 'Begin therefore with little things. Is a little oil spilt or a little wine stolen? Say to yourself, "This is the price paid for peace and tranquility; and nothing is to be had for nothing."'

It might seem a rather gloomy way to live, contemplating mishaps every morning as the intellectual equivalent of getting out of the wrong side of the bed. But the practice belies an underlying optimism. On the whole, Stoics believed, things in life work for the good. This is what emerges when you honestly examine life more closely. To put it another way, Stoicism can be thought of as another version of the common ancient Greek assumption about the necessity of accepting things. In the Cynics' case, that acceptance was purely pragmatic: if you can accept things, you will be happier. In the Stoics' case, it is worth learning to accept things because they believed the world is, in the final analysis, benevolent.

This is a crucial part of Zeno's rationale for the benefits of philosophical training. It is the foundation that makes sense of learning to withstand pain and nurture your own happiness by considering the worst. The whole process might be summed up as learning to go with the flow. Discerning the flow begins within yourself, understanding the nature of your feelings, for example, and how they can toss you about. As you gain some inner harmony, your mental life becomes clearer and you can learn to cultivate that. Finally, as you become a more proficient Stoic, you will realise that nature as a whole is as measured as you have become; for your nature is only one part of the whole.

In fact, Zeno thought that nature as a whole is divine, or supremely good. That is why you can trust his way of life. Another Stoic, Chrysippus, described life as being like a cylinder. It will be subject to various forces and tugs, for that is what it is to be alive. But you have a choice. You can either live resisting those forces, or you can live in harmony with them. The art of living is to shape your soul so that it is like that of a perfectly circular cylinder, one that can absorb the knocks. The reason you might want to do that, apart from making life easier, is that to refuse these forces is to construct a barrier between yourself and nature, and so distance yourself from the excellence of the cosmos. Similarly, contemplating the worst in the morning is about avoiding being so preoccupied with the minutiae of life that you miss the best during the day.

Epictetus offers another example of this philosophy of everyday life. He asks how a Stoic should deal with the feelings aroused by missing a bargain whilst out shopping.

It is a common experience. He imagines being in the marketplace, at the vegetable stall, and seeing the person in front of you being given some lettuces for free. However, when your turn comes, the stall-keeper changes his mind and charges you one obolus. The question is what should you do about the rage that results from the sense of injustice, petty though it might be? How should you respond to having to pay for your lettuces?

One response would be to forego the lettuces. In that case, reasons Epictetus, you keep the obolus that you have not handed over, and have lost nothing. What's to worry about? Another response would be to pay for the lettuces and take them. In that case, you would have paid the right price for the lettuces, so again you have no grounds for complaint. Moreover, you have something to eat for supper. A third response would be to accuse the shopkeeper of being unfair and go on the attack. But that would be irrational – he or she is under no obligation to offer you a bargain – and would only cause you mental disturbance. 'If you would at the same time not pay the [money], and yet receive the [lettuces], you are unreasonable, and foolish,' Epictetus concludes.

Such domestic scenarios are not unusual in discussions of this philosophy. Although Stoics often used dramatic examples to make a theoretical point, they stressed that it is in the little things of life that you must practise the right attitudes. If you wait until the wave is sweeping over you, it will almost certainly be too late. So although they talked about torture and committing suicide, they believed that it is in the many trivial moments of existence that you train yourself to deal well with the few tremendous moments. There really is no such thing as a trifling ethical question. Hence the importance of shopping.

This, perhaps, explains something else, namely how Zeno's philosophy got its name, Stoicism. Its ethical training has much to do with what might be called the marketplace of life, and suitably enough it began in the marketplace. The name comes from Zeno's habit of teaching in a stoa – the ancient Athenian's shopping precinct – and in particular the colonnade known as the Portico of Pisianax. 'You will find everything sold together in this place at Athens,' wrote Euboulus, a comic poet of Zeno's time. 'Figs, witnesses to summonses, bunches of grapes, turnips, pears, apples, givers of evidence, roses, medlars, porridge, honeycomb, chickpeas, lawsuits, beesting puddings, myrtle, allotment machines, irises, lambs, water clocks, laws, indictments.' Recent excavations in the city have revealed the

Figure 17 Another reconstructed stoa, of Attalus, Athens (Photo: Alaniaris)

foundations of a stoa on the north side of the Agora that archaeologists reckon to have been the one in which Zeno taught.

All in all, Zeno was drawn to shops because they provided a rich source of incidents to work on. When people are engaged in financial transactions, they reveal much about themselves, and who you are as a person is precisely what interested Zeno. He was comfortable with places of trade too, of course; it was in his blood, as the son of a merchant, and as a merchant himself. Philosophy first came to him because of the gifts his father bought on his travels and then brought home. When he first arrived in Athens, Zeno immediately went to a shop, a bookshop. He didn't have to think twice about that. It therefore comes as no surprise that he set up in the stoa to sell his philosophy, and it worked as a location for that too.

Stoicism lasted for six centuries, became the philosophy of choice for many Romans, and was borrowed by the Christians when they came to formulate their ideas about ethics. Epictetus' writings were used in the training of monks. In short, the Stoics knew what modern psychologists of consumerism know too, with their databases that track your habits: there's a lot you can learn when out shopping. Shopping – how you respond when you don't get the deal on the lettuces you wanted – casts a spotlight across your whole life. Reactions at the deli are quite as illuminating as any psychometric test. So the shops can be an excellent place to deepen your philosophy of life – to shape your character in preparation for the rarer moments when you feel you will be drowned by a wave.

It is said that after his remarkable suicide, by holding his breath, citizens clubbed together to build Zeno a tomb in the Kerameikos, or pottery district. You can walk those streets today, as they have been uncovered, and cast an eye across to the Acropolis. It is a peaceful spot, patterned with boundary stones, tombs, low walls, grass and pretty flowers. Imagine it differently though, buzzing with potters and prostitutes, travellers and traders, and philosophers. You can catch a glimpse of the bourgeois life that Zeno saw as his training ground. We say shopping is a religion. He would have said that philosophy provides us with the resources to examine this central part of our lives.

CHAPTER 10

Aristippus the Cyrenaic and a common misunderstanding about pleasure

Hedonism is a philosophy of life that has regularly appeared throughout history. It would certainly seem to be one that is alive and well today. It needs little explanation and can be summed up as the pursuit of pleasure, or at least the reduction of pain. It has an immediate appeal since pleasure is so nice. Hedonists don't need to commit themselves just to simple pleasures, such as food or sunshine. They can advocate the value of sophisticated pleasures too, such as reading or friendship. But the advantage seems to be that not only is this philosophy self-justifying, it is an easy one to live by too. Ask what you should do, and you opt for the choice that yields the most pleasure.

Only, is it that simple?

Aristippus the Cyrenaic is our man here. He was one of the first who is remembered to have put the philosophy to the test, for he lived it to extremes. Unlike the principle by which Epicurus lived – less is more – Aristippus adopted the opposite. He truly and fundamentally made pleasure the beginning and end of life. It determined his every choice. He even refused to delay gratification in the hope of receiving a greater pleasure later, as a more modest hedonist might. That, he argued, was to risk losing out on the pleasure that the here and now can give. He wanted it all, and now.

So it is worth asking how he managed it, and whether this philosophy of life really works.

Aristippus could claim an impeccable philosophical pedigree: he was one of Socrates' intimate circle. And it is perhaps for this reason that part of the tradition remembers him with a kind of affection. They see him as something of a loveable rogue, and feel he was a bit of a Falstaff. For example, he was accused of being a turncoat and a poodle, to which he

Figure 18 Book plate of Aristippus

unashamedly replied that he wanted an easy life. What has philosophy taught you, he was asked? 'The ability to be at ease in any society,' was his reply – which, in a way, is no mean achievement.

Other sayings wittily capture the philosophy of the Cyrenaic:

> If it were wrong to be extravagant, it would not be in vogue at the festivals of the gods.
>
> It is better to be a beggar than uneducated; the one needs money, the others need to be humanized.
>
> I came to Socrates for education and to Dionysius the King for fun.

There was some subtlety in all this too. The easy life, he argued, is not just one of pleasure. It is also one that is lived in the present. What is the point of being a hedonist who constantly longs for things, who pines after what he has not, who wishes his life away? And living in the present is not as straightforward as the injunction sounds. Most live in the future or the past, and so hoard their possessions or worry about their luck. Aristippus sought to demonstrate what it takes to overcome these anxieties in some of his remembered, or perhaps apocryphal, actions.

One day he was hungry. So he went to purchase a fowl, and emptied his pockets for the gamekeeper. It turned out that his pockets were full, which meant that he paid wildly over the odds. Onlookers asked what he was doing? The money is nothing to me, Aristippus replied: all that I know is that I'm hungry. That's called being in the present.

Another day, his slave was carrying the money for him, and found that the purse was too heavy. Most aristocrats would have had the boy whipped. Aristippus cried: 'Pour away the greater part, and carry no more than you can manage.'

A different kind of 'presentness' was shown on another occasion, when he was presented with three courtesans as a gift, and asked to pick one for his pleasure. He took all three, with a crack about seizing the day.

Needless to say, this kind of extravagant behaviour attracted not just verbal criticism but violence. The person who lives his life to excess quickly attracts the approbation of the self-righteous. Some spat in his face. Wiping off the spittle, he retorted that a fisherman does not complain if he gets wet pulling his catch, so why should he? And he could give as good as he got. When accused of charging money for his time, he replied that he did not charge for his own sake but so as to teach his students how to spend the cash. Another time, one young man came to him bragging of the amount he could drink. Surely he was a hedonist too? A mule can drink as much, Aristippus snapped back. Another flirtatiously boasted of his diving prowess, suggesting Aristippus might indulge in another kind of pleasure, perhaps with him in the pool. He put the lad down by asking what's so good about diving? Dolphins do it better.

Figure 19 Lid of coffin from the so-called Tomb of the Diver, Paestum

One final anecdote. One day he was being shown around an expensive house by the steward of Dionysius the King, a man called Simus. Simus was known for being a rogue, though not of the loveable type; more Iago than Falstaff. He officiously told Aristippus to take particular care when walking on the costly tessellated pavements. The mosaic was worth a fortune, more than Aristippus could ever afford, Simus implied.

At that moment, Aristippus felt the phlegm shifting in his throat. He needed to spit, but where? Not on the floor of great price. The perfect solution to his predicament struck him in an instant. He spat in the face of Simus. The steward was outraged and protested. 'I could not find any place more suitable,' Aristippus sneered.

It was a free life. It was also wittily iconoclastic. But at the end of the day, the way of life advocated by Aristippus the Cyrenaic was more critiqued than it was celebrated. So why?

Xenophon provides a clue. He composed a scene in which Socrates himself chastised Aristippus for his life of luxury. A life led purely for pleasure is a life trapped by lasciviousness, says Socrates:

> For example, quails and partridges are attracted by the cry of the female because of their desire and expectation of sexual intercourse and, losing all count of the risks, rush into the hunting nets.

The remark is almost certainly fabricated, but it is clear what Xenophon thought of Aristippus' hedonism. To be compared with a rushing partridge was a low blow. More substantially, the image suggests that uncompromising hedonists will quickly find themselves trapped in all sorts of tangles. The pursuit of pleasure will trap them, much as, say, the addict becomes a slave to his or her habit. Or the problem might be that they get

caught up in a vicious spiral, seeking ever more intense pleasures, when the body can only take so much; it's the fate of the
sixty-year-old rocker who can never grow up. Alternatively
again, a life of pure pleasure seems simply unsustainable,
because most people must also make at least some time to work,
or because the pleasures this world has to offer are ultimately
limited. The disappointments of consumerism prove as much.
These, as we saw, were the kind of points that Epicurus made.

It seems that Aristippus was mistaken about Socrates from the
start. He was drawn to the great man not because he'd heard
about his wisdom, or because of some personal quest, but simply
because Socrates was famous. Aristippus wanted to bask in
some of the reflected glory, to brag that he knew him. Things
rapidly went wrong. For example, Socrates was well known for
not taking money for his teaching, believing that wisdom should
be shown to be beyond price. Aristippus didn't get it, and went
around collecting money for Socrates. The sage refused it.

But the element that truly worried him was not the silly mistakes like that. Rather, it was that Aristippus represented a way
of doing philosophy that if established would have destroyed
the whole project to which Socrates, Plato and the like were
committed.

For one thing, hedonism can be seen to unravel under the
weight of its own contradictions. Sooner or later arises the
question of which pleasure. The apple or the pear? The lover or
the friend? The hedonist then becomes embroiled in 'felicific
calculus', as the eighteenth-century hedonist Jeremy Bentham
was to call it. The problem is that these pleasures cannot be
compared since they fundamentally differ. Hence as a philosophy at least, hedonism falters.

In addition, the goal of the hedonistic life is the achievement
of a state of careless enjoyment. If Aristippus sought an

easy life, he sought an easy philosophy too. He argued that it should aim at happiness, but unlike others he reduced his concept of happiness so that its total content was pleasure, good-feeling. With this schema in place, virtue would have little to do with right insight and would become nothing more than the capacity to indulge in sensuousness. That takes some doing, as the stories about Aristippus suggest. However, it replaces the struggle for sagacity with the immediacy of satisfaction. It dethrones wise living as the object of the philosopher's life, and puts pure indulgence in its place. Shakespeare's Falstaff eventually comes up against Hal, and the words with which Hal rejects his former companion in *Henry IV Part I*, could equally have been said by Socrates in rejecting Aristippus:

> ... there is a devil haunts thee in the likeness of an old fat man; a tun of man is thy companion ... Wherein is he [Falstaff] good, but to taste sack and drink it? wherein neat and cleanly, but to carve a capon and eat it? wherein cunning, but in craft? wherein crafty, but in villany? wherein villanous, but in all things? wherein worthy, but in nothing?

Wherein worthy, but in nothing? That is the charge against the hedonist.

Another point added to the case that Aristippus was beyond the pale. Like other philosophers of the time, Cyrenaics regarded themselves as citizens of the world. They travelled around the Mediterranean as many others did. However, they took that freedom to imply that they did not belong to any one state. This was, in a sense, a reaction to the times. Whilst citizenship had been closely tied to participating in a particular city-state – in its voting or juridical procedures – the city-states of the Mediterranean had fallen into a parlous state, and after Alexander they ceased to exist. Cyrenaics might have said they were wising up to the times. Globalising forces uproot individuals and the wise move is to embrace the upheaval and enjoy the ride.

Most, though, regarded this attitude as an abnegation of responsibility. It was leaching off the glories of Greece and putting nothing back. As the scholar Wilhelm Windeband described it, theirs was the 'philosophy of the parasites'. They might be rather like the fat cats of today, who enjoy all the benefits that nation-states provide, but themselves live on offshore retreats where they don't have to pay any taxes.

For all of the objections, Aristippus found a following and the Cyrenaic school lasted for a while. Hedonism will always have an appeal. However, the successors to Aristippus soon manifested its internal contradictions too. Theodorus, the first, abandoned Aristippus' dedication to the pleasure of the moment, in favour of having a cheerful frame of mind. He thought that was a better philosophy. Until Anniceris, another disciple, shifted it again. He argued that spiritual pleasures, such as friendship, were superior to carnal enjoyments, such as sex.

Hedonism can actually lead to a kind of pessimism, and not of the constructive sort of the Stoics. The logic here is that if you cannot decide which pleasure to enjoy, then maybe you should aim a little lower, and simply decide on the best strategies to avoid pain: if you can't identify the good, then at least avoid the bad.

Anniceris' fellow student, Hegesias, took this route. He concluded that there was only one real way to ensure a painless life and that was to dedicate yourself to complete inaction. Further, there was only one way to be resolved to inaction, and that was to kill yourself. He wrote a book with the cheery title *Death by*

Starvation. Amongst the students of Alexandria, where it was published, it became a must-read. Several apparently took his advice quite literally, which led the pharaoh to ban it. Hegesias the Death-Persuader, as he was known, provides the sternest warning to the would-be committed hedonist. It is surely no coincidence that the modern world has seen outbreaks of student suicides, too.

But where does this leave us in relation to pleasure? Surely the lesson of Aristippus and his followers is not that a life of no pleasure is the best life? It is not. In fact, Socrates himself clearly enjoyed the pleasures that life afforded, not least the joys of friendship. Or there's Plato who set one of his greatest dialogues, the *Symposium,* at a drinking party. Aristotle too, when he wrote about happiness, noted that the enjoyment of pleasure is integral to the concept, and desirable in life. And there's Epicurus.

So their criticism of Aristippus was this: the mistake is to make pleasure your sole goal in life, as if hedonism were self-justifying, as if life were so simple. If you do adopt that philosophy of life, pleasure will be your undoing, sooner or later. Rather, they thought, we should enjoy life's pleasures when they arrive, and not yearn for them when they go. That way, they can be appreciated for what they are. Moreover, if you seek instead to live a moral life, then pleasures will naturally follow. For, they suspected, happiness and goodness go hand in hand.

CHAPTER 11

Onesicritus hears the call to live more simply

When Henry David Thoreau committed himself to a two year experiment of living simply, in a self-built wooden hut on the north shore of Walden Pond in Massachusetts, he was responding to a call that most people hear at some point in life. In a word: simplify. When it comes, it sounds like the sure route to all things good. 'I wanted to live deep and suck out all the marrow of life,' he writes in his memoir of that time, *Walden*, 'to drive life into a corner, and reduce it to its lowest terms, and, if it proved to be mean, why then to get the whole and genuine meanness of it, and publish its meanness to the world; or if it were sublime, to know it by experience'.

The difficulty is that modern living is not simple. We own far more than the three chairs to which Thoreau restricted himself – 'one for solitude, two for friendship, three for society'. To test simplicity's promise, to stop the sense that life is being frittered away in a thousand trivialities, to seek out something more basic and rewarding, you have, therefore, to perform some very dramatic, almost violent, act – as Thoreau did when he moved into the shack. (That said, he still had someone who

visited to do his washing and bring some meals.) It is not a decision most are able to make. We may go backpacking in our
youth, tasting the freedom of cutting back solely to what we
can carry, but most return home after a few weeks and pick up
where we left off with work, with worries, with the accumula-
tion of stuff. When we face times of uncertainty, a related feeling may come upon us: a quiet sense of gratitude for the
relative hardship. It can act as a reminder of what really matters
– though the bust is soon forgotten when the boom times
return, as they nearly always do.

So mostly, those who have heard austerity's call do not fundamentally change their lives but instead find some space for
simplicity amidst the complexity, in activities ranging from
planting a few vegetables in the garden to mending their old
clothes rather than discarding and replacing them. Insofar as
they go, those activities are not to be belittled. They can genuinely nurture the ability to pay more careful attention to the
world, another of the joys that simplicity brings.

The Cynics, the followers of Diogenes whom we left on the
streets of Athens, came to fascinate the Greeks, for the very reason that they simultaneously repelled them. And it was all to
do with their radical simplicity. They lived like dogs, eating out
of their hands, sleeping in the dirt, copulating in a shady colonnade, indecently cursing passers-by. This way of life spoke to
the shadow side of the proud ancient Greek psyche, the part
which recognised that whilst their civilisation was great, such
progress came at a price. The Cynic's way of life spoke of the
uncluttered alternative, and although most would never
choose it, they nonetheless found it compelling.

And yet even the Cynics felt there was more they should be
doing to drive life into a corner, to reduce it to its lowest terms.
Moreover, there were rumours that there existed a group of

philosophers who lived an even more extreme life than they. Could that be true? What challenging truths did they expose? What unsettling spectacle did they promise? The rumours came along old trade routes from the East. Novel ideas as well as tasty spices had long passed up and down these highways of exchange, though to most Greeks, the origin of the alien intellectual currents was as mysterious as the source of the Nile.

That changed in 327 BCE. It was then that Alexander the Great mustered his largest army, perhaps 120,000 men, and pushed into the ancient country of India. Henceforth, the East would become more transparent to widespread Western curiosity. And amongst his entourage was one Onesicritus.

Onesicritus was born on the small east Mediterranean island of Astypalaea. Today, this member of the Dodecanese is almost forgotten, at least by tourists. Its beaches are covered with seaweed; its hills are bleak and windswept. Sheep and goats

Figure 20 Alexander the Great fighting at The Battle of Gaugamela, eighteenth-century relief

outnumber its inhabitants. In antiquity it had a stormy reputation too. Its most famous son, the boxer Kleomedes, was remembered for being disqualified from the Olympics when he killed an opponent. Enraged, he rushed back to his island-home, demolished the local school, and killed all its pupils in the process.

Onesicritus left the island on the back of his skills as a sailor, becoming a helmsman in Alexander's navy. At some point he had also become a student of Diogenes, and was therefore knowledgeable about philosophy and the Cynics too. He came to India with Alexander, not because of his seamanship, but in order to study the systems of thought that Alexander's expeditions encountered – much as a Victorian captain who was also an amateur naturalist might find employment collecting the local fauna and flora.

We know Onesicritus enjoyed the privileges of being close to Alexander's inner circle because he later became an advocate of the theory that Alexander was poisoned when he died. So maybe he also advised the great man to spend some time at Taxila, the place Pyrrho had visited before.

There was little there to otherwise attract a conqueror. Though the town was located at the crossroads of three trade routes, it consisted of not much more than a wide main road, around which were gathered mudbrick buildings with flat roofs, single slit windows and packed-earth floors. There was just one public building of wood for Alexander to process to. However, Taxila's sun-baked slum exterior concealed other sources of intrigue, perhaps even riches. It was an important centre of Vedic and Buddhist learning, and hence was a home to those exotic philosophers who 'out-cynicked' the Cynics, the naked philosophers or the Gymnosophists.

Alexander's party found them in the marketplace. They appeared to come in two varieties, one wearing long hair, the other cropped. Sitting in the dirt, dogs close by, they were observed to anoint locals with oil and, in return, were offered honey and figs, gratis. Food led quite naturally to conversation. They were treated with great respect and honour. Rich and poor, men and women alike welcomed them into their homes.

Curiosity sparked, Onesicritus was dispatched to seek out their leader. He dutifully rode out from Taxila and after about half an hour came across another fifteen such wise men. They were exotic enough to excite any philosopher, not just on account of their nakedness. Some were squatting, others sitting, others lying. All adopted bizarre yogic poses. One, who the Greeks came to call Calanus, was in the habit of balancing on one leg whilst holding a wooden beam about five feet long. When he could no longer maintain his indifference to the agony of this posture, he would nonetheless continue by swapping to the other leg. Diogenes himself had not thought of doing anything like that.

As Onesicritus approached, this Calanus called out – with an insult. He ribbed the Greek for wearing a cloak, hat and boots in the heat. Laughing, he continued, rehearsing one of their ancient myths:

> In olden times the world was as full of barley-meal and wheaten-meal as now of dust; and fountains then flowed, some with water, others with milk and likewise with honey, and others with wine, and some with olive oil; but, by reason of his gluttony and luxury, man fell into arrogance beyond bounds. And Zeus, hating this state of things, destroyed everything and appointed for man a life of toil. When self-control and the other virtues

in general reappeared, there came again an abundance
of blessings. But now, the condition of man is again close
to satiety and arrogance, and so probably everything
will be taken away.

Onesicritus was told that he must take off his clothes, and sit
with them naked on the hot stones, if he wanted to hear more of
their teaching. He told them not to be insolent, though another
Gymnosophist, called Mandanis, remarked that Onesicritus
was the insolent one, imperiously striding into their country
and making demands. That said, the Indians had heard of
Alexander. And it seems they respected him although he was a
soldier. After all, Onesicritus' presence was proof that
Alexander did not just seek new lands but wisdom too: he
played the philosopher-in-arms as well as the king-in-arms.

A conversation followed. East met West – though then as
now and as before, the dialogue was hampered by the difficul-
ties of translation. The language problem was particularly felt
because the Cynic and the yogis did not seek merely to
exchange pleasantries. They wanted to see how their philosophies were related. That was a complicated business and without a decent grip on each other's languages, it was like
expecting clean water to run through mud, Mandanis
observed. Did they sit on the hot sand and suffer being cooked
in the sun for the same reason? Did their embrace of extreme
asceticism yield the same insights? Was it necessary to be so
extreme to live so simply? And who was the more extreme
anyway?

Onesicritus reported back to Alexander. His report was in
turn recorded by the historian Strabo, and scholars believe it
may echo Onesicritus' own words. The Indians, he said,
believed that the key to it all was to free the soul from pleasure

and pain. Pain is bad. Hardship, though – what one might call voluntary pain – is good. Submitting the body to such practices somehow leads to understanding.

This last thought was a new twist for the Cynics. Diogenes and his followers lived in barrels, ate out of their hands and even masturbated in public as a way of demonstrating the freedom of simplicity. They, thereby, showed that they thought their fellow citizens were imprisoned by the complicated business of civilisation. In other words, ancient Cynicism was nothing if not a philosophy for the city. It rejected that which is called civilised, though of course Cynicism itself needed civilisation to react against. Only by reacting to its opposite, its other, could they know they were living simply.

The Gymnosophists had freed themselves even of that. They'd become convinced that hardships had value in themselves, regardless of their prophetic worth. They fought an internal war, not one between different ways of living in the world. Their nakedness and meditative poses focused on that which was inside themselves. The Indians peered into the nature of such experience itself and found there the birthplace of insight. If the Cynics spoke the truth to the powerful, the Indians spoke the truth to themselves.

That the Greek Cynics had not taken this final, and to the Gymnosophists, fundamental step was revealed to Mandanis when Onesicritus resisted the prospect of sitting naked. It suggested he still held on to certain customs. The yogi insisted that he must push through even that shame to truly understand what they were about. Mandanis put it this way: he said the Greek philosophers had made an error 'in placing custom before nature'. That would have been an 'ouch-moment' for the Cynic, for it was precisely custom that they strove so hard against. You need to get back to nature to find real simplicity, is how we might put it. What could be more natural than naked-ness, the dress that nature provides?

Such a call speaks to our ambivalent feelings about simplic-ity, I think. On one level, it sounds extreme – overly romantic, tasteless or just impractical. And yet, on another, that it sounds extreme suggests that the challenge of simplicity, and the promise it might hold, remains alluring, if basically beyond us. Are we not tied to the city, and civilization, like Onesicritus? I think that is right. Most do not live in shacks by Walden Pond. So what more can be made of it? Is there something that we can still take from it? I think there is. And it can come from the prophets who are still around us, and who pick up from the Gymnosophists. Here's one I happen to know of a little, Chris Park.

This is a picture of him in his home-crafted coracle, carrying a magic egg. He took it the length of the Thames, as a symbol of his unity with nature. Chris lives an extreme life. He would

Figure 21 Chris Park (Photo: Kirsten Manley)

agree with Thoreau: 'A man is rich in proportion to the number of things he can let alone.' His home is in the Vale of the White Horse, England. Much of his time he lives outdoors, though he shelters in a yurt, gathering wood from a nearby copse to heat it, where he also finds water from a spring.

He has a smiling face beneath frizzy hair, though you sense a steeliness and seriousness behind the happy countenance. His teaching is that your hearth is your altar, your work is your worship, your service is your sacrament. He tells ancient stories, sings sacred songs. He believes he is preserving a way of life that will be of immense value after climate change does its worst, which will come about because the 'condition of man is again close to satiety and arrogance'.

It is tempting to criticise Chris and the ancient Gymnosophists, to come to the safe conclusion that he and they are simply mad. However, that would be to miss an opportunity. If we don't turn our backs on them, and instead can appreciate their witness, their call to live simply can be taken as an invitation to think again about the way we live, to ask once more how we might live deep and suck out more of the marrow of life. By their striking efforts to examine themselves, they may help us to examine ourselves too. Onesicritus left the Gymnosophists pondering that question, even though he couldn't stay with the naked philosophers. We might leave Onesicritus doing the same, maybe more determined to live a little more simply once again.

CHAPTER 12

Cleanthes the Water-Carrier on working so hard you miss what you want

There is a proverb which states that work expands so as to fill the time available. The late twentieth century has confirmed the point. This was the era in which the ultimate labour saving device appeared on the scene, the computer. And yet, all it has achieved is the conjuring up of more work. Those now ubiquitous, insistent blocks of text, emails, are the obvious case in point. According to one IT research firm, you are counted as *not* addicted to emails if you check your inbox just once an hour. Most look for new messages every few minutes.

That said, if the ever expanding nature of work is a feature of the networked age, it seems it was not an entirely unfamiliar concept to the ancients too. We know this because some of the Greek philosophers worried about what it might mean.

Cleanthes was one. He arrived in Athens, from Assos in Asia

Minor, with only four drachmas to his name – roughly four days wages for a skilled worker. He had been a boxer. Now, aged fifty, he wanted to wrestle with life and ideas, so he sought a sage. First he had to find work, for unlike many ancient philosophers, he had no other means.

We do not know what brought him to this point in life, presumably some kind of existential crisis. Not that it defeated him. Quite the opposite: it left him highly motivated. He went out into the city and found employment in a garden, lugging water, fertilising the soil and digging. Thus, he became known as the water-carrier. Then, he found Zeno in the stoa, and during the day, sat at his feet. He returned to his work at night so as to save his best hours for his new and greatest love.

He quickly became known and admired for his industry and for the energy with which he overcame his poverty – although some could not quite believe it. The authorities in particular became suspicious. On the one hand, they saw him sitting about all day in the Agora, in no apparent destitution. But on the other hand, he was observed writing notes on the blades of old spades for he could not afford anything as smart as papyrus. So they asked, how does this fellow earn a living? Is he up to no good?

They brought him to court to check out the legality of his income. Cleanthes had to call the gardener he worked for and the women who sold him the bones he ground into meal to feed the soil. They proved his story and testified to his character. The judges were so impressed, they voted to give him ten minas – roughly three months wages for a skilled worker. Not a bad return, given the handful of drachmas he'd arrived with, though he gave most of the honorarium to Zeno, his master.

His philosophy was straightforward. Don't work for more than you need when you have enough to support you in what you really want to do. Why? Well, money for money's sake turns you into a slave. Moreover, money appeals to the most powerful instincts in us – the desire to be secure, to own things, to feel superior. But these aren't necessarily the best instincts in us, those qualities of life that the philosopher seeks because to have them is to live the good life.

There was a rich tradition of discussion about work available to Cleanthes as he developed this philosophy of life. It reached back to Hesiod, the poet of around 700 BCE. He had struck a positive note in his seminal text *Works and Days*. Although, as he observed, labour is man's lot, he also noted that work brings many practical goods with it, such as food for the belly, activity to combat sloth and wealth to sustain a decent quality of life. So do work, Hesiod advised:

> that Hunger may hate you, and venerable Demeter richly crowned may love you and fill your barn with food; for Hunger is altogether a meet comrade for the sluggard. Both gods and men are angry with a man who lives idle, for in nature he is like the stingless drones who waste the labour of the bees, eating without working; but let it be your care to order your work properly, that in the right season your barns may be full of victual. Through work men grow rich in flocks and substance, and working they are much better loved by the immortals. Work is no disgrace: it is idleness which is a disgrace. But if you work, the idle will soon envy you as you grow rich, for fame and renown attend on wealth. And whatever be your lot, work is best for you, if you turn your misguided mind away from other men's property to your work and attend to your livelihood as I bid you. An evil shame is the needy man's companion, shame which both greatly harms and prospers men: shame is with poverty, but confidence with wealth.

Figure 22 First pages of Hesiod's *Works and Days*

That said, by the time of Cleanthes, a distinct ambivalence had crept into Greek attitudes towards work. The people who 'mattered', which is to say the senior members of the citizenry, were mostly aristocrats and had private means. They did not have to work and, further, tended to look down on those who did. Much as a rich playboy might sport a red Ferrari through the centre of town, incurring the envy or spite of his fellows, so the wealthy of ancient Athens would take a favourite white stallion into the marketplace for an ostentatious trot.

Whether or not you were the proud owner of a horse, everyone looked down on those at the bottom of the working heap, the slaves, the engine of the ancient Greek economy. As Aristotle so confidently asserted, slavery existed because there were some human beings who had something slavish in their nature; such individuals are not made to be free but to be led by more rational men. Aristotle realised that slavery was demeaning. He was glad it was not his lot in life. He feared having his liberty taken away and being sold into slavery, perhaps as a result of war, as most people must have done during the times in which he and Cleanthes lived. However, Aristotle didn't make the empathic move which is more or less natural to us today: it apparently never occurred to him that slaves in general might be lifted out of drudgery, the meaningless cycle of their labouring lives, and so find some dignity.

Artisans such as potters, shoe-makers and gardeners fell in between the extremes of moneyed aristocracy and penurious slavery; their skill was valued for its usefulness. Socrates, for one, took this thought a step further. He recognised that artisans possessed a kind of wisdom – the practical intelligence of their trade. That was, he argued, a kind of art, by which he meant that their know-how was embodied in their character. These were not skills that could be picked up just by reading a book. They were nurtured by following a master craftsman. Therefore, he suggested, it is not just their knowledge that should be valued but they themselves too, as people. Artisans, then, were not thought slavish. And perhaps they felt like many who work today: what they do for a living provides some sense of fulfilment, some sense of pride. However, what they are conscious of lacking is the genuine freedom that the ancient Greeks, at least, associated with the luckiest of men.

There was another category of 'worker' that is worth inserting into this taxonomy of ancient labour, that of the beggar, for they flag up another attitude to earning a living that some have had. In antiquity, as in medieval Europe too, there were individuals who were what can be called 'ritual beggars'. There were begging boys, women and priestesses who were associated with religious cults. Alternatively, troops of beggars might arrive at your house and serenade you, promising plentiful wealth and many children in return for a generous hand. It was a respectable activity, and for this reason: beggars called other people to account by unsettling the natural tendency to place your trust in your riches. My state could be yours, they said, as they looked you in the eye and held out a filthy hand. Or maybe, more gently, they reminded you not to work too hard.

Could the wayfarers and homeless today play such an honourable role for us again, and not just be regarded as a nuisance?

The Cynics picked up on this tradition. In their campaign to call people back to what mattered, they wandered about without possessions – bar a cloak, staff and satchel. Their strong conviction was that nature will provide and that humans are basically good, and so will help out too. Giving to these prophets of the road was therefore an opportunity to show your admiration of them. To be generous to them was to risk opening yourself to their way of life and perhaps benefiting from its wisdom – even if that came at you in the form of uncomfortable abuse. Epictetus the Stoic, who admired Cynics, painted this picture of them:

> I wear a rough cloak now, and I shall have one then. I sleep on a hard surface now, and I shall do so then. I shall also get a bag and stick, and I shall begin to go around begging from people I meet and abusing them.

There is a faint echo of this activity in George Orwell's thought from *Down and Out in Paris and London*.

> A beggar, looked at realistically, is simply a businessman, getting his living, like other businessmen, in the way that comes to hand. He has not, more than most

modern people, sold his honour; he has merely made the mistake of choosing a trade at which it is impossible to grow rich.

All that said, one should not paint too rosy a picture of such a life. There is a story about Diogenes the Cynic practising begging before a statue. When asked what he was doing, he said he was hardening himself to rejection.

Cleanthes the Water-Carrier was not begging. It was necessity that drove him to work. However, he was quite clear that whilst you should work if you have to, you should also do no more than you must.

We can capture a sense of this philosophy from the man himself in the only fragment of his work that survives. It is a 'Hymn to Zeus', and begins by extolling that great god, the First Cause of all things, the Ruler of the Law, he who sees the cosmos spinning in its course. Then, a few sentences on, the hymn becomes more personal. A sense of Cleanthes as an individual emerges as his paean takes on a reflective, moral edge:

> some are eager for fame, no matter how godlessly it is
> acquired;
> others are set on making money without any orderly
> principles in their lives;
> and others are bent on ease and on the pleasures and
> delights of the body.
> They do these foolish things, time and again,
> and are swept along, eagerly defeating all they really
> wish for.

Here is a phrase that still speaks across the centuries: they are swept along, those who make money for money's sake, 'eagerly defeating all they really wish for'.

This is what Cleanthes would have us avoid. He would have us realise that, actually, many are in a position to work far less. Moreover, if they do, they will have enough to pursue what they love and the time to do it. He worked to earn a living, and no more. And when more came his way, he gave it away. Few will do as Cleanthes did. Perhaps some of us should. Weaning yourself off those emails might be a place to start.

But there is the related element in Cleanthes' life that mustn't be missed. He knew what he loved, namely philosophy – discovered as a result of his midlife crisis. This is what brought him to Athens to sit at Zeno's feet. To put it more directly, he wanted to work less not for its own sake but in order to pursue his keenest interest. The deeper insight, then, is that you need to know what you love if you don't want to miss something in life – and moreover, love it enough to make the sacrifices of income and status for it. Knowing what you love may be more difficult to discern than it seems. Our next philosopher is of use when thinking more about how.

CHAPTER 13

Hipparchia of Maroneia on marrying for love

The life of the ancient Greek woman was, apparently, one of dreary domesticity and chaste commitment. The story goes that she was confined to her house, no freer than an enclosed nun. When she did venture onto the streets – perhaps to offer virtuous sacrifice for the protection of her husband and children at the temple – she was covered and escorted, subject to a regime of public reserve that would meet the approval of the Taliban. One of the reasons ancient Greeks might have been so fired by the firm flesh of young men was that womankind was simply not thought a fitting object of seduction, courtship and gallantry. Youths were to be wooed; women merely to be married. Lads had charm; ladies had children.

It was arguably worse for aristocrats. The higher your position, the more Byzantine the etiquette, and the farther you had to fall.

Andromache was the consort of the noble Hector. She is remembered as a tragic figure, condemned to mourn the death of her husband who was brutally killed and desecrated in the

Figure 23 *Andromache Mourning Hector* by Jacques-Louis David

Trojan war. In Jacques-Louis David's picture, she sits beside
the corpse in a cavernous interior, the luxurious home that is
her gilded prison. She gestures to her husband with an open
hand. She raises her eyes to the heavens. Sitting passively in her
loss, her child clinging to her drapes, all she can do is curse the
gods for her fate – as a victim of war, as a woman.

In her happier days, here's how she describes her practice of
marital modesty, according to Euripides' play *Trojan Women*.

> First, if a woman does not stay in her own house, this
> very fact brings ill-fame upon her, whether she is at fault
> or not; I therefore gave up my longing to go out, and
> stayed at home; and I refused to admit into my house the
> amusing gossip of other women … Before my husband I
> kept a quiet tongue and modest eye; I knew in what mat-
> ters I should rule, and whether I should yield to his
> authority.

And those were her happier days.

And yet, where there are rules, there are rules to be broken; where there is authority, there might be rebellion. If Andromache kept the gossips out of her home, that implies there were gossips forging their conspiracies, only elsewhere. And the ancient world did throw up a scattering of spectacular women who challenged the conventions of their times. Some of those were female philosophers.

Hipparchia was one. She was born in Maroneia, a city in Thrace, a region of northern Greece. It was famous for a wine that was said to smell like nectar and be of such resilience that it could be mixed with twenty times its volume in water. Dionysus, the god of the vine, was worshipped at Maroneia. There was a sanctuary in the place. The foundations survive, and suggest it might have been built in Hipparchia's lifetime. Coupled to the political upheaval she saw around her, perhaps a Dionysian devotion inspired her sense of rebellion, her conviction that she must pursue what she really wanted in life.

According to Diogenes Laertius, it all came to a head when the time drew near for her to marry – which is to say, the time to commit herself to who or what she really loved, and to learn who or what that might be. She would clearly have made a fine mistress to any well-heeled master, and she had many suitors. They processed before her, making a show of their wealth, high birth and handsome features. She was unimpressed and turned her back on them all.

Her parents were not pleased. They pleaded with her to be sensible, but their daughter dug in her heels. She said she would rather kill herself than fawn before these strutting peacocks. They perhaps spoke to her of how riches can encumber a life, overloading it with vanity.

But Hipparchia's wilfulness was not without another cause.

The truth was that there was already a man in her life. He was called Crates. He too was from a rich family, only he had become a social disaster. His story went like this.

One day, he had watched a play about Telephus. This mythical and tragic figure, a son of Heracles, had been injured by Achilles and the wound would not mend. Instructed by an oracle that his only chance was to persuade the one who was the cause of his distress to heal him, he doffed his honour, donned the rags of a vagrant, and stole into the camp of the Greek army. There he pleaded for mercy from Achilles his assailant.

The story moved Crates profoundly; it must have caught him at a suggestive moment though it's far from clear why. Whatever the reason, the story led him to spurn a substantial inheritance of 200 talents, an amount that would have made him a millionaire in today's money. He turned to philosophy – the unsociable dog-philosophy of the Cynic – and gave the cash to the poor.

The renunciation won Crates renown, of sorts, captured in a nickname, the 'door-opener'. Apparently, in his new life, he developed the habit of making rowdy calls on his fellow citizens, throwing open their front doors, before entering and admonishing those within. 'Wealth amassed is prey to vanity,' he used to preach, as the disturbed neighbours wondered how their wealth might be best deployed in the entertainment, or ejection, of the uninvited guest. It was not just that the rebuke made them feel uncomfortable. For an ancient Greek, as for many today, his home was his castle. A man might be challenged in the marketplace; that was only to be expected as a citizen. But to be personally censured in your private dwelling felt more like an insult. No doubt, the doors were sometimes thrown open again, as Crates was thrown out. On the other hand, some thought that the presence of the prophet, if inconvenient, might also bring good luck. Another of his nick-names was 'the good demon'.

It was this Crates with whom Hipparchia fell in love. She was enraptured by his bravery, delighted by his iconoclasm, drawn to his integrity. Aristocratic life had promised her merely the monotony of marital monogamy. In Crates, she found some-one and something she could give herself to with a passion. She did not want to spend a single day 'wasting further time upon the loom'. He was what she loved, along with everything he stood for. She was ready to make the necessary sacrifices.

At first, her parents were bemused. It was not just the shame. He was as ugly as sin to boot. The ancient Greeks could be bru-tal about bad looks, and Crates had grown accustomed to being laughed at, say whilst exercising unclothed in the gym. He comforted himself with the thought that in time everyone is tortured by sagging skin and aching joints: people laughed at him only because they could not face the truth about them-selves. There's a thought for a world in which cosmetic surgery is a growth industry – a sign that we can't face the truth about our mortality?

However, for all his rationalisations, the mockery must have had a profound psychological impact upon Crates. When he found out that the beautiful Hipparchia loved him, it was said that he stripped off in front of her, revealing his frame. Deformity is what I will bring to the marital bed, Crates was saying: if you can love me at all, it must be for my mind. I'll bring you few pleasures, though you can join me in a simple way of life.

Beast stood before Beauty, and Beauty rushed forward in embrace. He was precisely what she wanted. Beneath the fleshy appearance she perceived something divine. If she was unsure before, now she knew what she loved. She was ready to give herself to it.

The nineteenth-century German novelist Christoph Wieland
wrote a series of courtly letters as if between Crates and
Hipparchia. He imagines Crates worrying that she may come
to regret her choice:

> But may not you be deceived yourself, my dear lady, if
> you make yourself so certain, that the love of an oddity
> like Crates will make you happy? Much also as my heart
> clings to you, and rich as is the enjoyment of life which I
> can promise myself with you, what will you think if I
> confess to you, that I cannot sacrifice even to you, who
> make so great a sacrifice to me, a single one of the whims,
> as the world calls my peculiarities?

She, though, is sure and joyfully insists and accepts:

> You doubt, dear Crates, whether I do not perhaps
> deceive myself, when I take it as quite certain that the
> love of such a singular person as you are would make me
> happy. Do not be anxious on my account; the gratifica-
> tion of my heart makes me so happy, that there does not
> remain with me either a feeling of privation, or a wish for
> any thing better.

Marriage was generally a matter for parents to decide, not children, but there is no record of Hipparchia's parents objecting any
further. They may have been moved by her sincerity, impressed
by her commitment. It is striking when someone pursues what
they love, even if you can't see why. Or perhaps they too were
tired of the conformity of their own positions, suspicious of social
complacency.

Evidence of this is that Hipparchia's brother, Metrocles,
became a Cynic too: the philosophical movement seems to
have inspired the whole family. In fact, Metrocles might have

been the first to tell Hipparchia of Crates, the good demon having virtually saved his life.

What might have happened was this. One day Metrocles so embarrassed himself before his peers that he felt he could never face them again. Wracked with humiliation and ignominy, he had locked himself in a room and threatened to starve himself to death. Crates came to his rescue in an act of pure compassion. The older Cynic brought the youth a meal made out of the tasty yellow seeds of lupins. He told him that he faced no disaster. Rather, his shame was a wellspring of wisdom; the experience could be interpreted as the birth pangs of maturity. It is how you respond to your blunders that counts, not the fact that you slip up. In fact, anyone who makes anything of his life is bound to make mistakes. Metrocles was amazed at this thought. He converted on the spot, and quite possibly rushed to tell his sister.

Hipparchia converted too. She embraced the life of her husband. Together, they went on to have two children, also raised as Cynics. This epigram, purportedly written in her voice, reads like her credo.

> I, Hipparchia of Maroneia, have not followed the customs of women, but with a manly heart I have abided by the ways of the Cynics. I have never been fond of the broach that fastens my garments, and neither have I been pleased with the bound foot and with the headband daubed with perfume. But a staff, and bare feet and whatever folded cloak clings from my limbs, and the hard ground instead of a bed, these I have chosen. My life is preferable to the life of the Menalian maiden, for hunting is not as good as seeking wisdom.

In fact, there is a double rebellion in this memorable marriage, this commitment to love. As a rule, the Cynics were against such conventional couplings for the very reason that they were so conventional. A later Cynic, Bion of Borysthenes – to whom we will come in a moment – condemned matrimony with cruel logic: 'If your wife is ugly, you'll have your punishment; if she is beautiful, you'll have to share her.' Alexandre Dumas' version of the sentiment sheds the overtones of patriarchy: 'The chains of marriage are so heavy that it takes two to bear them, and sometimes three.'

Unless, that is, you marry for love, well considered. Such a soulmate becomes another self to you, and together you are more than one. You can overcome all ideologies, even those that reject attachments, and discover a deeper kind of freedom. This suggests another thought, one worth contemplating in an age of common divorce. The point would not be the moralistic one, that people should stay together through thick and thin. In a sense, Hipparchia herself rejected that idea about marriage when she refused to marry the men who were originally lined up for her. Rather, her life demonstrates what sounds like a falsehood today, which is that commitment itself can be a kind of liberty. Conversely, endless choice can be a kind of bondage – again, as Hipparchia must have realised when the aristocrats of Athens paraded and displayed before her, begging her to choose them. Her commitment freed her to live the life that she wanted to live, and it was a good one too.

What this tale suggests is that loving what you want is so difficult because it is depends on having courage and the prerequisite of sure convictions. It is not just about feeling or romance. It is not really about romance at all, if you marry a Crates. Hipparchia's life highlights how costly it is, though it is a price that sets you free.

CHAPTER 14

Bion of Borysthenes and the wisdom of changing your mind

One thing that is striking about the most notable ancient philosophers is that they were often outsiders. It is true that Plato was an aristocrat, at home amidst the glories of Athens. And that Socrates was born and raised in the place, and rarely left the city, it was said. But then again, he had little inherited wealth, gaining more from his wife in marriage, and so he must have felt like an interloper amongst the rich young men who were his followers. Aristotle, as we've seen, could rarely have ever felt truly at home as he was often on the move for reasons of personal safety. And when we consider Diogenes, Epicurus and Zeno the trend seems firmly set. They were all foreigners in Athens, as were many of their first disciples, characters such as Onescritus and Cleanthes.

It was partly a product of the times. For whilst geopolitical upheaval brought personal risk and social unrest, it also brought opportunities to travel. As during other periods when globalising forces were at play, the world became something of a melting pot, and that is productive of new philosophies. Today we see something of the same, as ideas from the Far East gain currency in the West, and conversely as Western ideas start to shape the consciousness of people living in places like China. That can be a cause of fear, the fear of strangers and alien beliefs. Fundamentalism is one way people react. It is the attempt to draw lines in the sand of your beliefs – be they religious or scientific; lines which cannot be crossed, and which never change, though they always do, of course.

And so a better, more honest and wiser attitude to cultivate is just that: a preparedness to change as you assess and weigh new possibilities. It's a harder path to travel. It's one that can win you enemies and critics. But it is one that is open to the opportunities represented by a fast changing world. It is not so much a question of pure choice, as if the good life is one that offers an endless selection off an à la carte menu of creeds. Rather, with discernment comes deeper commitment, in the effort to live life to the fullest.

Our next philosopher is a model case in point. Bion was born an outsider and his life seemed destined for obscurity, if not disaster. His father, a dealer in salted fish, suffered during an economic downturn and fell into debt. His mother was a prostitute: they deserved each other, Bion said. When he was still a child, the whole family was sold into slavery.

Borysthenes, his hometown, could be found on the north coast of the Black Sea. To the Greeks it was virtually the end of the world. The name means 'wide land', referring to the endless empty steppe that surrounded it inland. Vastness was part of the consciousness of the place since it was also situated close to the mouth of the immense River Dnieper – also called the

Figure 24 Bust, thought to be Bion, found in the Antikythera shipwreck

Borysthenes. At over two thousand kilometres in length, it is the Mississippi of the Ukraine.

That said, when Herodotus visited in the fifth century BCE, two hundred years before Bion was born, he concluded it was a veritable cornucopia:

> [Borysthenes] furnishes itself the most beautiful and most well cared for pasturages for cattle and the pre-eminently best and most fish, [it] is the most pleasant to be drunk and flows pure beside turbid bodies, while by it the best sown produce is produced and the deepest grass.

There were oddities about the town, and things to be marvelled at, Herodotus continued. Local delicacies included antacaeans, large sea creatures without spines. Its coins were minted in the shape of dolphins, not disks. But two centuries later, everything had changed and the place was in decline.

Delicacies could no longer be afforded. The market had collapsed, even for salted fish, hence his father's debt. Bion had double the reason to feel he was an outsider. He was born in a backwater and had become a slave.

However, he had one saving grace: good looks – or as he put it himself, he was 'a not ungraceful youngster'. Maybe part of his grace stemmed from the fine mind that lurked behind his visage. On the slave market, he was bought by a rhetorician, someone who made a living from pleading causes, and so could appreciate burgeoning intelligence. Bion must have impressed. When his owner, the rhetorician died, he left Bion every dolphin-shaped penny he had.

A child of fate, he knew this was his chance. The world was opening up and he must open up to it. He resolutely turned his back on the past. He burnt all his books, and in what sounds like a rite of passage, he bitterly intoned a line from Homer: 'This is the stock and this the blood from which I boast to have sprung.' He shook the Ukrainian dust from his feet. He was bound for Athens, a new life and philosophy.

Now, when someone shows impressive resolution, that can be interpreted as arrogance – one danger for those who make changes in life. Sure enough, when Bion arrived in Athens, some saw that as the defining characteristic of this upstart ex-slave immigrant from a dodgy part of the world. Diogenes Laertius calls Bion 'a shifty character', 'a subtle sophist' – which is as complimentary as calling someone a cunning lawyer. He was regarded as pompous, and those who were against philosophers in general – 'who are they to tell us how to live?!' – took to holding Bion up as an example.

The principles he adhered to perhaps help expand on why he made such enemies. He once accused a flirtatious young man of being as steady as a soft cheese left in the sun, implicitly criticising the louche tendencies of certain Athenians. He chastised another for taking secret pleasure in the ill-fortune of his friends, a characteristic of amity no-one likes to have highlighted. He was asked by a wealthy man about the causes of suffering, to which Bion replied, being wealthy: he explained the answer by pointing out that the trouble with wealth is that you do not acquire it, it acquires you. The psychology of the outsider is to see through much of what other people take for granted in life, and in particular to see its emptiness and conceits. Bion's 'mistake' was speaking his mind. He suffered as honest foreigners do.

Belittling money was a constant feature of his life. Later, under the patronage of the Macdeonian king, Antigonus Gonatas, he asked for three obols to buy some bread. The king gave him the whopping sum of a talent, which Bion handed over in its totality for the single loaf that he wanted. Perhaps that's what comes of growing up in a place where the coins are shaped like fish. Or it might be the behaviour of someone who has travelled, literally and in his mind, and so knows that money has no worth in life except for what it can bring you.

He also taught that giving gifts to others is better than receiving them for yourself, on the grounds that giving builds character, whereas receiving makes you passive. And he had a version of the saying that narrow is the way that leads to life, commenting that the road to Hades is easy to travel.

All that would have been enough to upset his despisers. But what really got under their skin was his claim to have integrity. Surely anyone could see that this traveller from the north was an intellectual Odysseus too. And they perhaps had a point, for he did appear to change his mind time and time again.

Before settling down to the life of the Cynic he had been a student of Xenocrates, the head of Plato's conversational

Academy, where it was taught that the good leads to God. Xenocrates was undoubtedly a wise man and a natural choice for anyone looking for a guru. He used to say things like, 'I have sometimes regretted speaking, but never remaining silent.' Only, Bion subsequently left.

Next, in an apparent volte-face, he became associated with Theodorus, who was called the Atheist, and about as far from Xenocrates' Platonists as could be. Theodorus regarded himself as a citizen of the world too, and travelled from place to place: it might have been an endorsement of the peripatetic lifestyle that appealed to Bion.

And yet, he did not last with Theodorus for long, next being spotted attending the lectures of Theophrastus who was the head of Aristotle's school of philosophy, the Lyceum, and another rival to Plato's Academy. He had apparently gone over to another side once more.

Bion was accused of being a flip-flopper. It was said that he decked his philosophy in a coat of many colours: who could tell whether he was now for the reds or the blues, or the greens or the pinks? He had apparently been for all of them. However, I suspect there was something deeper going on. For he not only *said* he valued integrity; his actions actually suggest he did.

Ancient philosophy was plagued by individuals who presented it not as an art of living but as the art of persuasion. What mattered to these sophists was not the search for truth or the life lived well. Rather, it was winning an argument. They prostituted philosophy for profit. They did not search for what was true. They cared for what makes cash.

Bion loathed this tendency. He would have delighted in the words of the poet William Cowper. In his poem, 'The Progress of Error', the eighteenth-century man of letters wrote:

As creeping ivy clings to wood or stone,
And hides the ruin that it feeds upon,
So sophistry, cleaves close to, and protects
Sin's rotten trunk, concealing its defects.

Bion became so disillusioned with the rotten trunk of philosophy, in the very home of philosophy, that he moved to Rhodes. He declared that he had fine wheat to distribute not poor barley. More dust was shaken from his feet.

In other words, he sat at the feet of different philosophers not because he couldn't make up his mind, or as if he just loved the endless choice. Rather, he wanted to understand how different people think – not by reading their books or assessing their speeches, but from within, by seeing how they participate in life. He was not interested in being able to say, 'I know what you think,' but in being able to share the deeper sentiment, 'I see what you mean.'

This meant he had to submit to different points of view, for a time, and experience what it was like to inhabit that worldview. Then he would know about it not by rational analysis but by personal acquaintance. Bion felt that close to the heart of living well was the capacity to practise the art of empathy, to make the imaginative leap into seeing the world from different perspectives. This desire is another capacity that outsiders can have, though they may also recognise it as a danger. Paradoxically, having sympathy for others can result in exactly the opposite sentiment being directed at yourself.

This way of life is not just a question of acquiring different intellectual experiences, like the tourist who treats travel as a kind of checklist and confuses seeing the Pyramids with knowing Egypt. It is important because it is the first step towards gaining a real education, one that results in discernment.

Roman Krznaric, a contemporary thinker who also puts the art of empathy at the centre of things, has said that empathy involves 'extending ourselves beyond our own ego and self-interest'. 'Extending ourselves' conjures up associations of growth, broadening and deepening. It means moving beyond the safe confines of your own knowledge, thereby being able to gain from the riches of others and the lives they have lived.

In short, it takes strength to practise empathy. It leaves you open to the accusations of duplicity that Bion the itinerant faced. Perhaps the greatest risk is that empathy might leave you feeling that you yourself know nothing much at all. Then again, the reward is that it leads to profound insight: Socrates himself had argued that the key to wisdom is not how much you know but having a profound appreciation of the limits of your knowledge. That can be gained through thoughtful interactions with others. Socrates too, Bion must have thought, was a philosopher of empathy.

Bion became so committed to this philosophical method that later in life he developed a technique for practising it. It was called the diatribe. Today the word is synonymous with a bitter attack or a blind rant, the kind of thing in which fundamentalists indulge as they seek to defend their lines. It manifests exactly the opposite spirit that Bion wanted to nurture.

In his own time, a diatribe was at once less aggressive and more illuminating. It was a deliberate exchange that had the intention of being mutually beneficial to all participants. Bion borrowed the notion and added a twist. His idea was that you should imagine yourself in the shoes of your opponent, or the position you did not fully understand. Then, when composing your diatribe, you should write them the best lines. It would become an exercise in empathy and would be of benefit to you.

It might convince you to accept something you had been resisting, or at the very least broaden your understanding.

We don't actually have any of the diatribes that Bion wrote, but we do have some from a follower, Teles of Megara. In one, Teles imagines a man arguing against Poverty. He fears poverty and so in the tradition of the ancient diatribe has Poverty tell him why his worries are misplaced:

> Poverty says, 'Why do you fight with me? Are you deprived of any noble thing because of me? Of temperance? Of justice? Of courage? You aren't in want of life's necessities, are you?

The idea is not to celebrate poverty per se. It is that the man might have his fears of poverty lessened. In the diatribe he imagines what it might be like to be poor, and sees that it wouldn't actually deprive him of any noble thing – of temperance, justice or courage. He might realise that poverty is not as bad as he thought, and so free of his fear, he'd be freer to live. In short, by posing rhetorical questions, and deploying a little satire and parody against yourself, Bion's diatribe helps you to focus on what actually matters.

Another common concern in his time was precisely the fate that Bion had suffered, that of being made an exile, perhaps as a result of being conquered by an over ambitious Macedonian, perhaps as a result of being sold into slavery. Teles of Megara addressed that worry in a diatribe too:

> From what goods or what sort of good things does exile deprive you? Those of the soul, or of the body, or of externals? Sound reasoning, proper conduct, does exile deprive you of these? ... Surely it does not deprive you of courage, of righteousness, or of any other virtue? And

> surely it does not deprive you of any bodily goods? Or
> are not health, strength, keen eyesight and hearing the
> same if a person is in a foreign land?

Sound reasoning, proper conduct, courage, righteousness, health and strength: it makes exile seem quite attractive. Bion could testify to that.

The technique of the diatribe has proved to be an enduring one. Throughout the ancient world, subsequent philosophers took it up. In the Christian period, it became a staple of the sermon – sermonising being not unlike 'diatribing'. The diatribe was given a massive boost again in the sixteenth century in one of its greatest practitioners, the French Socrates, Michel de Montaigne. The diatribes that had been sermons became essays in his hands: in these pieces of writing, Montaigne assays or challenges himself. They sound fresh in our ears precisely because he addresses his real fears and personal concerns. Take this extract, when he asks how much it matters that in your actions you are consistent. It matters very much, might be a first reply, since consistency is the essence of authenticity. Well then, reflects Montaigne, take a look inside yourself:

> Not only does the wind of contingent things move me
> according to its own inclination, but in addition I move
> and disturb myself by the instability of my stance: any-
> one who turns his prime attention to himself will hardly
> ever find himself in the same state twice … I speak about
> myself in diverse ways: that is because I look at myself in
> diverse ways. Every sort of contradiction can be found in
> me, depending upon some twist or attribute: timid, inso-
> lent; chaste, lecherous; talkative, taciturn; tough, sickly;
> clever, dull; brooding, affable; lying, truthful; learned,
> ignorant; generous, miserly and then prodigal.

Figure 25 Michel de Montaigne by Daniel Dumonstier

The lesson is not to worry so much about this 'whirring' and 'discordancy'. It is wisdom to acknowledge it, and merely ignorant to deny that you change in the name of being consistent. The philosopher who realised the value of empathy would have agreed with that insight. In fact, Bion could have written Montaigne's essay himself.

Bion's wisdom – the insights he gained by trying to understand those who differed from him from the inside – was eventually recognised by some. When he fell ill, and it became apparent that he would die, the local king first sent him two servants to nurse him, and then he came to pay his respects in person. The man from Borysthenes made peace with his gods, those beings who do not know the joy of changing their minds because they know everything already. The colourful life of the many coloured philosopher drew to a close around 245 BCE. In a plural and multicoloured world today, his philosophy can live on.

CHAPTER 15

Menippus of Gadara on the seriousness of laughing

A cheeky smile hangs on the face of Menippus, as painted by the Spanish artist, Velazquez. He looks out at the viewer, half turned away, a sizable chickpea nose separating saucy, knowing eyes that dare you to follow him. He wears the clothes of a commoner, a heavy black cloak that reaches from his shoulders to his breeches and boots. Velazquez is reminding his patron, the Spanish king, of the philosopher's conviction that wisdom can come from the most unlikely of sources.

That source, in the story of the life of Menippus of Gadara, is laughter. Apparently, his books overflowed with humour, and so he brings us to another element in the art of living as described by the ancients. It turns out to have been a central concern.

This is perhaps not so surprising. Philosophy, it might be said, teases the mind. So, in a way, it is all a kind of elaborate joke. Think of something like the 'problem of the liar',

Figure 26 *Menippus* by Diego Velazquez

attributed to a philosopher of the fourth century BCE, Eubulides of Miletus. If I say, 'I am a liar', then presumably that statement is itself a lie, in which case I speak truth, so I can't be a liar. But if I speak truth, then the statement 'I am a liar' must mean I'm lying, so I'm not a liar at all. Ironically, the serious business of philosophy might, in part, serve as a reminder not to take yourself so seriously. Laughing at the limits of reason would be of value to human beings because it keeps them light about life.

Aristotle was probably the first to note that human beings are the only animals that laugh: 'No animal laughs save Man,' he wrote. The implication is that those who don't make merry – or worse, can't – are somehow less than human. Pythagoras risks being one of these: he was remembered by some for never laughing. Maths can do that to a man. Conversely, others were remembered for being perpetually amused. Democritus is the obvious candidate as he was called the 'laughing philosopher'. He cackled at everything from people's funerals to political elections, the

Figure 27 *Democritus* by Hendrik ter Brugghen

implication being that he saw the absurdity of life. That he found it so amusing was given as the reason that he lived for 100 years. This suggests a second reason to put a little laughter into your life: it delivers longevity. In fact, modern psychology has confirmed something a bit similar as optimistic people are reportedly much less likely to die of heart attacks than are pessimists.

Being philosophers, the ancients attempted to find theories that could account for humanity's strange habit. Plato proposed one idea as to why people laugh, usually called the superiority theory. He wondered whether people find things funny mostly out of malice: laughter is a result of the mixing of pleasure and pain in the soul. 'How many Platos does it take to change a lightbulb?' 'That depends upon what you mean by CHANGE.' The joke is at the expense of the philosopher, hence the 'superiority' tag. It serves to keep the sage in his place, mockery of the great and powerful being a third value humour can have.

Not that Plato was against it. His dialogues are known for their subtle wit. In fact, scholars have spilt much ink over what is known as 'Socratic irony'. It seems to have been implicit in the philosophical way of life that he ascribes to Socrates – the kind of humour, say, that draws friends together and helps to keep them more honest. He was aware that jesting could be used malignly too, when it seeks to refute an opponent with a cruel joke; sarcasm as the lowest form of humour. He was against that. Alternatively, Plato deployed what might be called tragicomic images to capture something of the human condition that serve to keep you smiling at it.

In the *Symposium*, he uses one as a kind of therapy for the heartache of love. Giving it to the character Aristophanes, who in real life was and is a well-known comic playwright, Plato writes that human beings were originally round wholes with four arms and four legs. They could tuck these appendages in and, like great balls, whizz across the face of the earth. The gods became fearful of these speedy and powerful creatures, and so Zeus cut them in two. This is how men and women were formed, the myth explains, each individual being a half of the original whole. Moreover, it explains something else, how now we spend our time on the face of the earth looking for our lost half, driven by the desire to recover a sense of wholeness. The therapeutic value of the myth is that it captures something both of the tragic nature of love, in the sometimes desperate need to find someone and to feel whole once more, and its comic nature, in the ridiculous image of the original, whizzing round wholes with four arms and legs. It helps you to laugh at the agonies of romance.

A related idea of humour is the incongruity theory. An example of this kind of witticism comes from an ancient joke book called the *Philogelos* (the 'laughter-lover'). It tells of a man who goes to the doctor complaining that when he wakes up in the morning, he always feels dizzy for about twenty minutes. 'Get up twenty minutes later,' the doctor replies. Cicero was helpfully to define the incongruity theory of laughter in this way: it is when 'we expect one thing and another is said; here our own disappointed expectation makes us laugh.' We have then another good reason to laugh: to save ourselves from discontent or distress.

Many of these notions came together in the life of Menippus. Born in the third century BCE, a slave who bought his freedom, he put his mark upon the tradition by noting that the dogged business of flouting customs and pursuing freedom is 'seriously funny'. He practised the studied art of the joker and became pretty influential, as having your portrait painted by Velazquez many hundreds of years after you died might suggest. In particular, he lends his name to a form of satire called 'Menippean'. These are prose pieces, almost like novels, that have as their target many objects of ridicule, but are distinguished by highlighting what has been called 'diseases of the intellect'. A famous example would be Apuleius' 'Golden Ass', in which the antihero is accidentally turned into a donkey as a result of an obsession with the practice of magic. The intellectual disease he suffers from is superstitious and irrational belief, at which the satire pokes much fun.

In a similar spirit are the stories about Menippus told by Lucian. The rich are a frequent object of scorn for Lucian's Menippus, and he derives keen pleasure from what will befall them. For example, he imagines the gods passing judgement on them, and as punishment, forcing their souls to reincarnate as donkeys for a quarter of a million years. (Donkeys and asses appear to have functioned in jokes much like chimpanzees and monkeys do for us: the ancient proverb 'Thistles are like lettuce to the lips of a donkey' could provoke spontaneous laughter when recited.) In another place, Lucian has Menippus mock the mumbo-jumbo practices associated with ancient Greek oracles – the way that the pious had to do things like throw cold water on a goat and watch to see if it would shiver, or don linen and hold a loaf before crawling on all fours into a cave. It was hocus-pocus to the lampoonist.

Lucian also writes the words that might be called Menippus' *credo*, a formula that gets to the heart of the value of laughter and summarises why it is such a valuable part of life.

According to the story, Menippus was searching for the meaning of life. He'd asked poets, politicians and philosophers, and they'd all proven to be precisely no help. Their sagacious speculations were wildly inconsistent. So Menippus went to a Zoroastrian Magus who told him that he must journey to Hades in order to consult the mythical prophet, Tiresias. Menippus armed himself with a lyre, a lion skin and a sailor's cap, in memory of the three individuals who had made that dark journey before – Orpheus, Heracles and Odysseus.

He entered and then travelled through the underworld, having a number of adventures on the way. And finally he catches up with Tiresias. He puts his question to the prophet: what is the meaning of life? And the blind sage has an answer. He leans over – Menippus is agog – and whispers these words into the philosopher's eager ear:

Arrange the present well and jog on, laughing a lot and taking nothing seriously.

CHAPTER 16

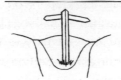

Marcus Manilius on the exercise of free will

There are some features of ancient life that don't hold sway today, some beliefs that were common then and just aren't any more. A good example of this is the notion of providence, the suspicion or hope that someone, or something, is playing a role in shaping your destiny. Apart from the most skeptical and hardened philosophers, everyone in antiquity thought twice before tempting fate. That fear has evaporated for the modern, secular mind simply because it is now thought never to have been real.

Some still hold out for luck, manifest in habits such as purchasing a weekly lottery ticket. Others have claimed the old powers of providence for themselves, arguing that people make their own luck. The idea of providence has changed even for religiously minded individuals, most of whom in the West at least would now believe that if God exists, he or she must be a merciful, just and fair divinity. A god who condemned people in the heartless way the Greeks and Romans envisaged would now be considered a deity who was less than human.

And yet, what is interesting about this profound shift in mentality is that echoes of the old way of thinking still survive. Its influence can be detected in certain ideas we have, even when they are strictly this-worldly. To see the role it plays, and how it affects the hopes and aspirations that now underpin our lives, a re-examination of the ancient conception can be illuminating.

One way into this area is to consider the life of Marcus Manilius. He is sometimes called the last of the didactic poets, the tradition of writing in antiquity that reaches back through the Roman Lucretius to the Greek Hesiod. Manilius had a great mind, coupled to an artistic nature. His five book poem, called *Astronomica* – the reason we know of him at all – places him in the vanguard of cosmic knowledge, as it was in the first century CE. (This is the period we have now reached in our journey through the lives of ancient philosophers.) For example, the zodiac system of houses, the division of the sky into twelve astrological units that supposedly relate to different spheres of life, appears for the first time in his book.

He has attracted major fans across the ages. Perhaps the most recent of note was the poet and classicist A.E. Housman. In one of his letters, Housman confesses to preferring Manilius to Aeschylus, and believes any decent Latin scholar would feel the same. Housman's edition of the *Astronomica* was a labour of love: he struggled to get it printed over a period of nearly thirty years.

The devotion is all the more marked since little is known about Manilius the man. However, one facet of his character stands out in the obscurity that otherwise surrounds him. He exemplifies a basic Stoic doctrine that was much debated in antiquity, and has been revived in philosophy today. That is the doctrine of determinism, the extent to which factors beyond our control shape our lives. It was heavenly powers that were

Figure 28 Manilius depicted viewing the heavens in a bookplate

thought to rule our fortunes then: providence. It is biological and physical forces that we presume do so now. But the interesting thing is that at least part of the question has remained the same: whoever or whatever the source, exactly to what extent do these factors rule us? To put it another way, how much freedom do we really enjoy?

Manilius took an extreme view of fate. He argued that even the most apparently subtle of our possessions, our thoughts, are determined. 'No they aren't!', you might retort in an attempted display of freedom – to which Manilius would reply that fate had predicted your response before you became conscious of it, before you started reading this chapter, perhaps before you were ever born. Just because you acknowledge your actions are determined doesn't make you any less subject to cosmic forces.

Today, a not dissimilar argument does the rounds. One prominent version of it concerns the nature of free will, a

capacity that would seem central to a good life. It is often discussed in relation to some experiments performed by a psy-
chologist called Benjamin Libet. He monitored the brains of
individuals as they moved their hands and bent their fingers. In
particular, he asked his subjects to signal to him when they
thought they were deciding to flex their digits. What he
discovered was that an unconscious part of the brain anticipated the conscious decision by remarkably long periods of
time – subsecond but still substantial. The conclusion that
many have drawn from these results, and others like them, is
that free will is a delusion. Prominent philosophers and scientists are now on record declaring that our brains decide these
things for us and so free will itself is dead. One less freedom for
humankind.

Now, there are good reasons to question such a speedy
judgement, to which we will return. But for now, let us
suppose that this strong determinism is right, that the liberties
we presumed were ours as humans are in fact conventions
or delusions. It is a theoretical view worth exploring because
it is increasingly common, and there'd be value in being
alerted to what would be lost to us if it were shown to be right.
We can do so by asking what philosophers like Manilius had
to say about the matter, for this is the belief they held. Why,
we might ask, given this view is right, did they still think life
was worth living? Is determinism not the worst kind of
fatalism?

The fascinating thing about Manilius and his fellow Stoics is
that this apparently dire situation did not provoke them to
despair. Quite the opposite: they thought determinism was not
a source of fear but of freedom.

Stoicism is fascinating for the way it balances fate and providence. Then, as now, some regarded these two elements as

opposites. 'Each man is the smith of his own fortune,' thought Appius Claudius Caecus, the builder of the Appian Way, that great monument to freedom. Exactly wrong, argued Virgil: 'The gods thought otherwise,' he wrote.

The Stoics were different again, since they held that the two coincide. They were fatalists but not fatalistic, fate being providential. For them, the great challenge of life was to discover and embrace your fate.

This 'optimistic determinism' stemmed from their philosophy of science. They were, at once, thoroughly naturalistic, believing that the forces at play in the material world can account for everything that happens; and yet, they were also devout believers, convinced that an underlying principle works through the forces of this world, steering all things for the good. They called it the logos or God.

The question is how to reconcile the two. Stoic fate is an endless succession of causes, and in such a cosmos there is apparently no free will. If an event seems lucky, chosen or miraculous, that is but an indicator of a deeper, concealed cause. The two are not incompatible they said. Seneca, the second-century Stoic, expressed it well in his letter, *On Providence:*

> Even the phenomena which seem irregular and undetermined – I mean showers and clouds, the stroke of crashing thunderbolts and the fires that belch from the riven peaks of mountains, tremors of the quaking ground, and the other disturbances which the turbulent element in nature sets in motion about the earth, these, no matter how suddenly they occur, do not happen without a reason; nay, they also are the result of special causes, and so, in like manner, are those things which seem miraculous by reason of the incongruous situations in which they

are beheld, such as warm waters in the midst of the sea-waves, and the expanses of new islands that spring up in the wide ocean.

So how can the universe be simultaneously administered by a purposeful mind *and* blind providence? What role is there for divinity to play? The Stoic solution to the problem was basically to say that the divine will and caused events are one and the same thing. Because God is rational, his will manifests itself as logical causes. It could not be otherwise, for that would be to imply that God were irrational.

Consider some more of Seneca's letter, for from this follows a stress that life is good. 'Nature never permits good to be injured by good; between good men and the gods there exists a friendship brought about by virtue.' And in that formula lies another element to his answer. The things that can befall individuals, which might be called evil, may well be hard in themselves. But they, thereby, nurture virtue in that person, and so, in that sense, can be called good. '[God] does not make a spoiled pet of a good man; he tests him, hardens him, and fits him for his own service.'

The result is resilience. Whatever befalls the tested and proven individual, tranquility is always their possession. And that is worth having. 'Just as the countless rivers, the vast fall of rain from the sky, and the huge volume of mineral springs do not change the taste of the sea, do not even modify it, so the assaults of adversity do not weaken the spirit of a brave man,' Seneca continues. 'Disaster is virtue's opportunity.' From which it follows that *good* fortune is the real enemy. It could even be called bad, inasmuch as it undermines the practice of virtue. 'Flee luxury, flee enfeebling good fortune, from which men's minds grow sodden.'

Figure 29 Bust, possibly of Seneca

Reading such justifications, it might seem that the alliance of fate and providence is bought at the price of a distinctly macho ethic. Seneca's metaphors are borrowed from soldiery and sailing: the bravest are the noblest; those most hardened to the waves are the best. However, there is a related strand in Stoicism that softens it.

This is the sense in which Stoics simultaneously learn to see themselves as in sympathy with nature, as acting in harmony with it. That enlightened view is quite as much a part of virtue as sheer hardiness. The philosopher becomes conscious of the logos as a living being, to which he or she is linked. Placing yourself within this divine order is a liberation. The training of virtue is a training for freedom, since it is to flourish in the way that has been ordained. 'I am not God's slave but his follower,' Seneca believed of himself.

So the tranquility thereby gained is not fundamentally based upon a brutish tolerance of pain and difficulty. At root, it is a spiritual contentment, which emerges when the individual learns to see the cosmos from the right perspective. That brings acceptance, and a rejection of the compulsion to forge the world to suit your desires and petty satisfactions. Seneca concludes: 'There is no unhappiness for those whom habit has brought back to nature.'

From the Stoic conception of happy fatalism expounded by Seneca, Marcus Manilius emphasised another dimension, a contemplative element. In fact, the driving spirit of his poem, the *Astronomica*, is a love of the stars, the lights that show how we can embrace whatever befalls us. Astrology is presented as the gift of the gods to guide us through this fateful world. The forces that link us to the planets were first discerned by the ancient Egyptians, and now, Manilius believes, the gods have provided new tools to enlarge on this science, namely the empirical methods of astronomy. Developments in magic and occultism are the concrete results of progress alongside the advances in technology and knowledge being made at the time.

His poem begins with a fiery cosmogony, an account of the origins of the universe. It reads surprisingly well, given our own scientific perspective, discussing how rotations in the heavens produce centrifugal forces, and how the planets and stars travel through space. Where his beliefs come through is in his conception of the cosmos as a living and breathing organism, of which the human organism is a part. This Gaia hypothesis is an expression of 'cosmic sympathy', and it is this element which turns the straitjacket of determinism into an exo-suit that strengthens the actions of humankind.

To look into the heavens, therefore, is both to read the mind of the world and to see your own future. See how the constellations arise with sublime regularity! Contemplate this immense display and note how no body deviates from its course! Celestial movement is the wonder of life writ in the skies! This order provides the grounds for Manilius' confidence that a liberating determinism structures our lives. Its upshot is a deep interest in astrology.

If the future is fixed then it can also be known, in the stars. He turned to the heavens to learn what to do, for a rational decision was one that aligned itself with the flow. To put it another way, astrology was a kind of therapy. If what will be, will be, there is no point in worrying about the future. In fact, worry is a sign that you are trying to impose your will on the world, to oppose fate. That is a fruitless expenditure of energy. It is to turn your back on freedom. It is to never quite live. Instead, trust providence, reach for the divine. That is the rational philosophy. Manilius continues:

> Man know thy powers, and not observe thy size,
> The noble power in piercing reason lies,
> And reason conquers all, and rules the skies ...
>
> Who can wonder that the world is known
> So well by man, since himself is one?
> The same composure in his form is showed,
> And man's the little image of the God.

Not all the Stoics embraced such divination with enthusiasm. Panaetius, a couple of centuries before Manilius, had doubted its efficacy and feared that it would bring Stoicism into disrepute. But he was regarded by his fellows as something of a heretic: if the heavens spoke of the logos, and the embrace of fate was the essence of the good life, then one might question the methods some use to divine what to do, but surely not divination as a whole. Cicero exemplifies this approach in a dialogue he wrote, *On Divination*. He acknowledges that it seems a little silly to believe that Jove himself has a hand in whether a crow croaks on the left or the right. But then divination is an art as well as a science. Discernment is of the essence.

Astrology was to have a long association with its scientific cousin, astronomy. Right into the eighteenth century, leading physicists remained interested in the movement of the stars for reasons other than pure science. When Isaac Newton published his laws of gravity and universal motion one result was an upsurge in astrological speculation. That may seem bizarre. But recall what Newton's law suggested: there is a mysterious force that locks heavenly bodies together. Moreover, it acts on any mass, achieving everything from holding the moon in its orbit around the earth to causing an apple to tumble to the ground. Action at a distance; nothing escapes its influence. Isn't such a force precisely what astrologers have always believed in? Newtonianism seemed to validate the notion that the position of the planets could determine the outcome of a life.

Serious science has rejected that as superstition now. Gravity just isn't that kind of force. It determines the motion of the stars but not the trajectory of our lives. However, as we noted already, determinism itself persists as an attractive proposition in parts of the scientific and philosophical community. Cause links to cause in an endless chain, Stoics such as Manilius affirmed. Much modern science does too. Moreover, science has shown itself to be enormously successful at explaining all kinds of things. There is a great temptation to believe it will eventually explain everything, enfolding the universe in a complete system of laws. This is the source of the new determinism and the reason the philosophy has returned with force.

Experiments such as those to do with free will have provided new impetus to the theory.

For sure, the inheritors of Manilius' determinism no longer gaze at the heavens to determine the nature of your character; instead they decode your genome. They don't believe that a divine logos lies behind the delusion you call free will, but they reveal the influence of other hidden forces when they place you in a brain scanner. This is an inward turn, away from the stars. That would be an obvious difference between then and now. But in some ways the underlying motivation is the same: the universe is shaped by an inescapable causal nexus – the logos for the Stoics, the laws of nature for we moderns.

However, there is another difference, and humanly speaking it points to something that would be far more crushing should strong notions of determinism be proven right today. For the ancient Stoics, the powers that drive the cosmos are benevolent. The logos was good. This is wholly unlike the mindless causal chains of contemporary determinism. The newer doctrine asserts that life is but a mechanism; that the elements of which it is composed are blind and without purpose. The poet A.E. Housman, who so admired Manilius, expressed it like this: 'For Nature, heartless, witless Nature / Will neither care nor know.'

That is a bleaker view of things. It is a philosophy that would turn us into sleepwalkers. It is truly fatalistic – and would be dehumanising, according to ancients like Manilius, who would otherwise share so much of the same worldview. The Stoics help us see what is at stake in any headlong contemporary rush to embrace determinism as if it were certainly true and so should be a guide in life.

And there are grounds for questioning such a move, beyond simply that of fear for what it might mean to be human. For one thing, as was already suggested, the contemporary experiments are far from conclusive. Consider again those to do with free will, and the bending of fingers that is anticipated deep within the brain. In fact, whilst the experiments are fascinating, they don't demonstrate that free will is dead. For example, the subjects in the experiments always bend a finger. If they sat there and involuntarily bent a leg when they thought they might move their hand, that would be impressive. But they bend a finger, in compliance with the instructions they'd agreed to follow. Which is to say that in some way or other they are exercising their free will. Moreover, even though the movement may be anticipated unconsciously in the brain, it is important not to forget that your brain is part of you. That 'whole you' is still deciding.

Arguably, a better position to adopt, then, is that free will is a 'tangled labyrinth', as the Renaissance philosopher Erasmus described it. If the experiments on free will, and the implication that we don't have it, seem counterintuitive, that could be for good reason: understanding the nature of our freedom requires much untangling and may well be impossible completely to grasp.

And there's something else that comes to light by remembering the ancient Stoics. We may no longer share their sense of a benevolent providence. That much is lost to many. But *only* that much. After all, we can still look at the heavens with Manilius and appreciate the immense display, arguably with a degree of understanding and subtlety he could never have dreamt of. There is much beauty in that. Alternatively, the Stoics believed that life was good not only because they believed in a logos, but because human beings are clearly capable of doing good too. Surely no-one would say that human beings are any less capable of acting well, nurturing virtue and pursuing right than they were in Seneca's day? So to the beauty of the heavens we can add the good done on earth. As philosophers and scientists continue the tussle over what's determined and what's free, Manilius prompts us to remember that there is no need – at least yet – to throw everything of human worth away.

CHAPTER 17

Secundus the Silent on the dangers of travel

The late 120s and early 130s CE were years of relative peace. A cultivated emperor, Publius Aelius Hadrianus, was on the throne. Hadrian had spent the first few years of his reign calming the empire, curtailing the centuries-old expansionist policy of the Romans, choosing instead to consolidate his domains. 'He lived for the most part at peace with foreign nations,' remembered the historian Cassius Dio. From the misty hills of northern Britannia to the dry reaches of the upper Nile, stability nurtured prosperity – and also a desire to travel.

The emperor himself found it difficult to stay at home, if the many years of his reign that he spent abroad are anything to go by. He had the itchy feet of someone who wants to see every part of the world except his own back yard. When he was forced to return, he made an impressive effort to bring the world back with him, constructing a massive villa at Tivoli outside Rome to house it all. The villa consisted of imitative recreations of the world's great architectural sites. He filled it with the statuary and decorations he found on his travels as only the billionaire tourist can. The villa was actually a town; it was larger than London was at the time. One ancient source describes it thus:

> He built up the Tiburtine villa wonderfully, in such a way that he could apply to it the names of the provinces and places most renowned and could call parts of it, for example, the Lyceum, the Academy, the Prytany, the Canopus, the Poecile, Tempe. And so that he might omit nothing, he fashioned even a Hades.

Travelling is a dangerous business. It can leave you discontented as a result of sojourning in places of rainbow exoticism when compared with the grey familiarity of your own neighbourhood. 'Travelling is the ruin of all happiness! There's no looking at a building here after seeing Italy,' says Mr Meadows, of a rapidly industrialising London, in Fanny

Figure 30 The Emperor Hadrian

Burney's novel *Cecilia*. Alternatively, it might change you. If you are the first member of a family to go to university you face a grave risk: you may receive an education, return from whence you came, and find that home has become strange to you, and you to it. From then on you are forced to live in a no-man's-land between your university town and your home town.

Something like this is what happened to another traveller in the second century CE, a man who is now known as Secundus the Silent. His father, possibly a carpenter, died whilst Secundus was a child. The youngster was sent abroad, and after many years travelling, he returned to his birthplace. However, arriving home, he had changed so much that he was unrecognised and – this is the crucial detail upon which the story of his life turns – he decided not to let on.

If he had been a graceful youth, we can imagine his adult figure as shabby, long haired and bearded. He had become a philosopher. As to his character, we can get some idea from how he could argue a case. One dispute he reportedly solved concerned the instigator of a riot. It had been decreed that the instigator should die, which seemed straightforward enough, except that the condemned man also claimed that he had put a stop to the unrest. This was problematic because it was customary to give peace-makers a reward. So the puzzle that Secundus was asked to solve was whether this wily individual, who had both started and stopped a riot, should be executed or receive recompense. He seemed entitled to both. Secundus asked which had come first, the instigation of the riot or its suppression. The instigation. So, Secundus concluded, first the penalty should be paid out to the man. After that, he could enjoy his reward.

That was witty and smart. But it was to be for what he didn't say that Secundus became widely remembered.

Some time after he returned, he decided to test a distinctly unpleasant thesis, namely that his mother was a whore. Maybe the fantasy behind the thought was some kind of Oedipal response to being sent away as a child. That there was something Freudian going on is supported by the way he decided to do it. He bribed his mother's maid, who arranged for her mistress to be seduced by none other than Secundus himself – now, of course, a complete stranger.

It must have struck his mother as an unusual kind of personal service. For one thing, the man before her was compelling not because of his looks but because of his words. Second, as soon as the incognito Secundus set eyes on his mother's breasts, he turned over and fell asleep. Losing the maternal breast is one of life's greatest traumas, psychoanalysis tells us, so perhaps to recover it is a tremendous consolation. Whatever the cause of this strange response, it might have saved the day. Only in the morning, the experiment went horribly wrong.

The two woke up, and Secundus decided that this was the moment to reveal he was the long lost son. Shocked at his return, and horrified at the results of her salacity, his mother ran out and hanged herself. Now it was Secundus' turn to be perturbed. Unwilling to blame himself for the tragedy, he instead heaped condemnation on his tongue, in token of which he took a vow of perpetual silence. He would never speak again, never risk deploying words, those darts of sound that had brought such tragedy. They can kill, it is said. The life of Secundus serves as a reminder of just how destructive they can be.

Posterity judged him well. His penance was deemed appropriate, and he kept his oath. In fact, he became a philosophical hero. The story evolved into a myth and spread all around the ancient world, from Syria to Ethiopia. It seemed to work on many levels. There was the danger of words. There were the dangers of returning to your homeland when you yourself have changed. There was also the danger of putting those whom you love to the test. In medieval Europe, Secundus became a kind of secular saint: over one hundred hagiographic manuscripts relating his myth survive to this day. It would have been possible to find some version of the story in any decent Byzantine second-hand scroll shop.

There is another part of Secundus' story that is worth including in our guide too. On account of his vow, he became famous in his own lifetime. This brought him visitors. And in the year 128, a particularly memorable one passed by: none less than the emperor Hadrian, who was on tour. As someone who loved the incidents and accidents of travel, it is not surprising that whilst in Athens, Hadrian sought an audience with Secundus. Or perhaps it is more likely that Secundus was summoned to an audience with Hadrian.

What is for sure is that the ancient world relished the chance of an altercation between an emperor and a philosopher. It had started with Diogenes in his barrel telling Alexander in his armour to step out of the sun. These were meetings between one individual who fought to maintain power and another individual who sought to undermine it. They fired the imagination because for all their differences, emperors and philosophers had something in common: both lived apart from normal conventions and rules – the emperor because he made them, the philosopher because he spurned them. They enjoyed a freedom that most didn't, and when they jousted, inconceivable power would bump up against intractable principle, promising something of a spectacle. The emperor had everything to lose, the philosopher nothing. Which kind of freedom would win?

On this particular occasion, we can surmise that Secundus had reason to be nervous. Hadrian was known for his temper.

Galen, the great writer on medicine, records the day an angry Hadrian lashed out at a slave with a pen in his hand. The poor man was blinded. Filled with remorse, it was only then that the emperor considered the ramifications of his rage. He demanded that the slave be compensated. The slave, in a moment of wry humour, asked for a new eye. What the powerful do can often not be undone. That is something worth remembering in life.

The restless ruler and the remorseful thinker met. Hadrian asked him to explain his philosophy, as it was recorded in a book, *Life of Secundus the Philosopher*, written about a hundred years after his death: 'Speak, philosopher, so we may come to know you. It is not possible to observe the wisdom in you when you say nothing,' said the emperor.

Immediately, there was an impasse. Secundus would not speak. So Hadrian pulled rank:

> Secundus, before I came to you it was a good thing for you to maintain silence, since you had no listener more distinguished than yourself, nor one who could converse with you on equal terms. But now I am here before you, and I demand it of you; speak out, bring forth your eloquence.

Still nothing.

Hadrian called for a tribune to exact some words: when you've a hammer in your hand, every problem looks like a nail. Except that this nail wouldn't budge. 'It is possible to persuade lions and leopards and other wild beasts to speak with human voices, but not a philosopher against his will,' commented the tribune, before declaring that refusing the emperor is a crime that can only be punished by death.

Still Secundus stayed mute. He enjoyed the perverse liberties of individuals who have done something of which they are so ashamed that they no longer care whether they live or die.

Secundus was immovable. He had no power in the world apart from his choice not to speak. Why should he give up the little he had? So he appeared before a now impressed emperor once more, and this time agreed on a compromise. He would write replies to twenty of Hadrian's enquiries.

Secundus' answers add up to a kind of catechism for the philosophical life. It is for what he reportedly wrote that he was no doubt also remembered. For example, Hadrian asked, 'What is death?' Secundus inscribed:

> Eternal sleep, the dissolution of the body, the desire of the distressed, the desertion of the spirit, the fear of the rich, the desire of the poor, the slackening of the limbs, the flight from and loss of life, the father of sleep, an appointment truly prearranged, the end of all.

Or there is his response to 'What is poverty?':

> A good thing that is hated, the mother of health, a hindrance to pleasures, a way of life free of worry, a possession hard to cast off, the teacher of inventions, the finder of wisdom, a business that nobody envies, property unassessed, merchandise not subject to tariff, profit not to be reckoned in terms of cash, a possession not interfered with by informers, non-evident good fortune, good fortune free of care.

But it was with the question 'What is the Universe?' that onlookers got the spectacle of power versus powerlessness they desired. Hadrian was answered by a Secundus who penned words – darts of sound – that must have pierced the emperor to the heart.

You, Hadrian, as it happens, are full of fears and apprehensions. In the bellowing wind of winter you are disturbed too much by cold and shivering, and in the summer time you are too much oppressed by the heat ...

Today is already passing us by, and what the morrow will be we do not know. Think not lightly, therefore, O Hadrian, of what I am saying. Boast not that you alone have encircled the world in your travels, for it is only the sun and the moon and the stars that really make the journey around it.

Secundus had seen the truth behind Hadrian's desire to travel. Psychologically, he could not stay still because he secretly feared death. By keeping moving, he did not have to pay attention to that which was closest to him, namely the shortcomings of his own life.

The memento mori was said to have affected Hadrian profoundly. As chance would have it, after 128 and the meeting, he had to cope with several personal and political disasters, first as a result of the death of his beloved in Egypt, then with the bloody Jewish revolt in Judea. He became less a voyager and more a fugitive, his compulsion to travel ceasing to be a joy and becoming more clearly the outer manifestation of an inner restlessness.

He did, however, honour the man who made silence a philosophical practice, and who understood the dangers of travel. Hadrian ordered that Secundus' books be deposited in a sacred library. As for Secundus, so far as we know, he did not leave his home town again.

CHAPTER 18

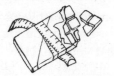

Sextus Empiricus and the folly of food fads

What we eat is a modern obsession: it has become commonplace in the West to observe that for the first time in history, affluence is leading to a shortening of the natural lifespan of *Homo sapiens* because of an outbreak of obesity. 'Our graves are dug more by our own teeth, ably assisted by knives and forks, than by those of predators,' muses Raymond Tallis grimly in his meditation called *Hunger*. That said, when we look, it turns out that diets and dieting have been a perennial human concern, at least in recorded history. The ancient philosophers were no exception and there is perhaps some consolation to be found in the fact that even those who aimed to live well thought a lot about food. So what did they think, and has their advice any relevance for our food anxieties today? One man's counsel is particularly apposite, that of Sextus Empiricus. But before we get to him and his times, which were the latter stages of the second century CE, consider some of the suggestions of his predecessors.

We can begin by remembering Diogenes the Cynic. On the one hand, he taught his followers that they could and should eat anything. After all, he argued, vegetables and meat, fruits and grains, wine and water, are all ultimately made of the same material stuff: 'All elements are contained in all things and pervade everything,' he averred, so there is little point in being pernickety. This isn't so much you are what you eat, as you might as well eat what you are. However, and on the other hand, Diogenes was also concerned about the tendency that rich foods have of encouraging human beings to indulge in culinary excess. So he thought that a diet of simple food and plain tastes were best. That is most likely to nurture a reflective way of life.

Stoicism, which grew out of Cynicism, argued that you should eat to live rather than live to eat: the natural demands of the body are actually pretty minimal, Stoics felt, and usually fairly easy to satisfy. More profoundly, they continued, life is characterised by a range of fascinating hungers that extend way beyond the physical – emotional hunger, intellectual hunger, spiritual hunger. So surely it is better to devote at least some of your time to pursuing these more interesting manifestations of your yearnings. To be absorbed merely by the question of what you eat is, in a sense, to turn your back on the deeper facets of what it is to be human.

In such a vein, Seneca argued that 'celebrity chefs' – the leading cooks of his time who were much in demand in Roman high places – were a sign of a degenerate culture. Feasting had become debauched. 'When we recline at a banquet, one slave mops up the disgorged food, another crouches beneath the table and gathers up the leftovers of the tipsy guests,' he notes in one letter to a friend. 'Another carves the priceless game birds; with unerring strokes and skilled hand he cuts choice morsels along the breast or the rump. Hapless fellow, to live only for the purpose of cutting fat capons correctly.' Little wonder that the affliction of our age, obesity, also troubled the aristocrats:

> The master eats more than he can hold, and with monstrous greed loads his belly until it is stretched and at length ceases to do the work of a belly; so that he is at greater pains to discharge all the food than he was to stuff it down.

Philosophy, in contrast, calls for modest living and eating. That is not just a question of good taste but common sense, Seneca continues: 'Food does no good and is not assimilated into the body if it leaves the stomach as soon as it is eaten.' He might have offered his support as a patron of the slow food movement.

The rival school to the Stoics, the Epicureans, also had something to say about food. Their founder, Epicurus, was the man who felt he was eating quite as fulsomely as Zeus when he took delight in barley-cakes and water. 'Send me a pot of cheese, so that I may feast whenever I like,' the advocate of less is more reportedly said.

Not that the Epicureans were averse to food. For one thing, they grew their own, in their philosophy schools that they literally called 'gardens'. Other philosophies taught that self-sufficiency was a good thing, but only the Epicureans tried it, and became self-sufficient in peas, cabbages and olives. Anyone who has held a seed in their hand and wondered at the enormous return it yields, just by being planted in the ground, has experienced the same sense of the earth's freely given fecundity as the Epicureans.

Epicurus thought well of another food-related exercise too: fasting. He fasted for what you might call experimental reasons, to explore the links between what you eat and happiness.

For measured periods of time he would only partially satisfy his hunger and then watch how a reduced or simplified diet affected his level of contentment.

There were two reasons Epicurus thought fasting was such a useful practice in the art of living. First, there is always the possibility of suffering should food not be available. In the extreme case, this would be because there was no food at all. Famines did rage periodically through Greece during the centuries in which the ancient philosophers lived. Athens was better able than many places to withstand the failure of the crops, or curtailments in the food supply because of wars. It had a port; grain could be shipped in from Egypt. Nonetheless, food prices varied wildly and cost might be another reason certain foods became beyond your reach. Thus, Epicurus argued, it was a handy skill to be able to take pleasure in the victuals that fortune might well snatch away.

That reason for fasting may seem to have lost much of its rationale in the developed world of the modern West: we could not be said to suffer from any significant shortage of food, or at least not yet. But there is another reason that Epicurus advocated fasting that hasn't dated, which is a simple curiosity about this desire which we call hunger.

Science has not quite pinned down the mechanisms that lead us to feel hungry, or full. The emptiness of the stomach matters to a degree, but so do blood sugar level, blood insulin level, the level of fatty acids in the blood and the body's temperature. There are external factors involved too, including catching a sight or smell of some tasty food – the 'bacon butty' phenomenon to which even the committed vegetarian may be susceptible. Pure habit plays a major part, such as tummy grumbles as the clock strikes lunchtime, or the compulsion to pass an otherwise empty afternoon by filling yourself with snacks.

Epicurus was interested in exploring these workings of his mind and body. Deliberately fasting, consciously observing the effects, assessing the variety of pains and pleasures, physical and psychological: food is an excellent locus for gaining the wisdom that is called self-knowledge.

That might be even more the case in a world where food is taken for granted. Fasting could be a practice whose time has come again, not just as a means of losing weight or practising self-control, but as a way of learning about ourselves and the culture in which we live.

And there is a related part of contemporary food culture to which the ancients might draw our attention too: the proliferation of diets. In the US, it is estimated that roughly one-third of men and two-thirds of women are on a diet at any given time. Dieting is quite as much a part of the food industry as the production of food itself. Whole cities are on diets, as in the case of Oklahoma City: the mayor made a New Year's resolution in 2008 that the population as a whole would lose one million pounds. The size of that figure is gross in itself.

Dieting has became something of a religion, as in the 'Christian weight-loss movement'. The videos, support groups and products marketed by the pastors and cheerleaders for this 'spiritual discipline' are mostly targeted at women. The crass theological justification for it goes something like this. God is your ultimate best husband, and he will find you sexier if you can offer him a decent shape. So ask, what would Jesus eat? Do thou likewise.

Secularists will chuckle, until they recall how often newspapers lead on similarly simplistic stories to do with dieting – one headline suggesting red wine is good, the next bad; one magazine advocating the benefits of stripping out carbohydrates, the next championing a gospel of balance. Why do publications

Figure 31 Sextus Empiricus from a medieval book plate

worry us about our waistlines? Why do contradictory 'experts' get fat on the newsprint? Diets sell.

So we come to Sextus Empiricus. He was a philosopher, a physician and above all a Sceptic: he joined the movement of philosophers who adopted the name meaning 'enquirers' or 'searchers'. They felt that accepting the limits of our knowledge, not celebrating the extent of it, was the wellspring of wisdom.

Sextus is actually our best source on the history of ancient Scepticism, the followers of Pyrrho. He tells us that as a way of life it was discovered almost by accident. The fathers of Scepticism were committed to the life of searching for truth, as is expected of philosophers, only they found they were unable to make much progress. Moreover, the struggle to say whether things were good or bad, right or wrong, left them increasingly troubled. Finally, almost out of exasperation, they struck on the idea of simply stopping the search and suspending judgement. And a strange thing happened: they were overwhelmed by a sense of contentment and tranquillity, as if storms had been calmed and strife had ceased. 'When they suspended judgement,' said Sextus, 'tranquillity followed as it were fortuitously, as a shadow follows a body.'

Sceptics still experienced unpleasant feelings, such as pangs of hunger and thirst. However, unlike most people, they came to believe that these were not necessarily bad things in themselves. Thus, whilst they continued to experience the cravings, they did not continue to suffer the additional dimension of believing they were bad feelings – as if they somehow should never have to feel hungry or thirsty, and that a moral wrong was being done to them when they did, or an injustice. Scepticism is a kind of acceptance of the way things are, good or bad. Therein lies its secret.

When it comes to the proliferation of diets, and drawing on this fundamental insight, Sextus could offer several reasons why they cause disquiet in the world, to say nothing of rarely helping people permanently to lose weight. First, he would note that there is no consensus as to what might constitute a good or bad strategy for shedding a few pounds. This confusion, he would continue, suggests why there are so many diets out there: it suits the dieting industry to ensure that punters have plenty of choice; a lack of consensus directly correlates with an increase in profits. Hence, dieting becomes a way of life for people whose weight remains roughly the same. As boom follows bust, so putting on weight follows taking off weight. Dieters don't become lighter, they become 'weight-watchers'.

If, though, they took a lead from the Sceptics, and suspended judgement, they might find some contentment. That might or might not lead to the loss of pounds, but it would lead to the lessening of stress: the very over-abundance of dietary advice has arguably become at least as great a problem as obesity.

Sextus was called 'Empiricus' because he followed the empiricist school of doctoring. It argued that it is often impossible to say why some cure, treatment or palliative works, though being a good Sceptic, Sextus was quite open to the possibility that an explanation could emerge at some point in the future.

In the meantime, when it comes to food and diets his advice is simple. 'Hunger conducts us to food, and thirst to drink,' so follow those feelings without shame. However, do so, not according to what the experts tell you, those who would lead you to extremes, but in accordance with 'everyday observance' – what we might call common sense. Bread, by all accounts, appears to be nourishing, so do eat some bread. However, don't overdo it, for it is also obvious that too much bread is unhealthy.

'People can choose food not merely and simply to have the largest portion, but to have the more pleasant,' Epicurus remarked in a similarly practical understatement, one to consider next time you are ordering from the menu. 'Take a little wine for thy stomach's sake,' is the sentiment again, this time deployed by Saint Paul.

CHAPTER 19

Hypatia of Alexandria on living in times of violence

Digging deep can be one response to social and economic upheaval, and the uncertainty and change the philosophers of antiquity faced undoubtedly played a substantial part in launching the project we call philosophy. However, one feature of this period of history that we have only mentioned in passing so far is that of violence, real and threatened. It is evident in our own times again: wars and atrocities are more or less as common now as they were then, and there is no sign they are about to disappear. In fact, if climate change proves to be as serious an issue as scientists like James Lovelock believe – he suggests that the seven billion-odd people living on the planet today will be cut to around one billion by the end of this century – then the conflicts of the past are going to appear trivial by comparison with what we will face.

So how did the philosophers address such violence? One story stands out as exemplary: that of Hypatia of Alexandria.

We are now in the fourth century CE. The Alexandria of Hypatia's day had reached the peak of its intellectual prowess. It was the sun around which other cities, mere planets of learning, revolved. If you go to Alexandria today, all that remains of this golden age are the faintest of echoes, carried mostly in the name. Occasionally, you might spot a fluted column or Ionian pedestal, standing isolated in a patch of green that serves as a traffic roundabout. The Pharos lighthouse astonished the world at 135 metres in height and could be seen for miles at night. This wonder of the ancient world now lies under the sea, or perhaps under the foundations of the grey high-rises that stand ominously, row on row, along the modern coastline like dominoes about to fall.

The philosophical hub of ancient Alexandria was the Mouseion, founded by Demetrius Phalereus, a follower of Aristotle. This building housed the famous library: it was extravagantly said to possess 700,000 scrolls and, as a 'copyright library', a complete set of the ancient Greek canon. It was not so much a museum as an institution that drew to itself the greatest minds of the age. Alumni included Euclid, Archimedes, Galen and Eratosthenes. Religious scholars contributed to its life too, including Jews and in the later Roman period of Hypatia's time, Christians, for believers and pagans typically studied together. It has been likened to Oxbridge, or the Collège de France, or the Institute for Advanced Studies. Hypatia was linked to the place by birth; Theon, a philosopher and her father, was its head.

Though few firm details of her life survive, it is clear that she was celebrated in her time. She was educated first by her father, and is said to have surpassed him in the mathematical sciences. She persuaded him to send her to Athens, and she spent a period there, wearing the philosopher's cloak. She studied Plato and Aristotle and could expound on both with equal

Figure 32 Portrait of Hypatia by the twentieth-century artist Elbert Hubbard

authority. She was awarded a laurel in recognition of her ability. Back in Alexandria, a tenth-century Byzantine document puts it like this. She was:

> as articulate and eloquent in speaking as she was prudent and civil in her deeds. The whole city rightly loved her and worshipped her in a remarkable way.

Her lectures were popular and she would have pulled crowds of worshippers when she took rides in her chariot through the streets.

The most reliable record of her life comes from the Christian chronicler Socrates Scholasticus:

> There was a woman at Alexandria named Hypatia, daughter of the philosopher Theon, who made such attainments in literature and science, as to far surpass all

the philosophers of her own time. Having succeeded to
the school of Plato and Plotinus, she explained the principles of philosophy to her auditors, many of whom
came from a distance to receive her instructions. On
account of the self-possession and ease of manner, which
she had acquired in consequence of the cultivation of her
mind, she not infrequently appeared in public in presence of the magistrates. Neither did she feel abashed in
coming to an assembly of men. For all men on account of
her extraordinary dignity and virtue admired her the
more.

We catch other glimpses of the affection and reputation she
enjoyed in a series of letters that were written to her by a student, Synesius of Cyrene, who later became the bishop of
Ptolemais. They are rich in human sentiment. In one, he writes
asking her advice about the publication of one of his books,
since only she is 'really able to pass judgement' about it. 'You
always have power, and long may you have it and make good
use of that power,' he continues.

She was admired for more than possessing beauty and good
judgement. She was the kind of person who could command a
deep and emotional loyalty. That speaks of a charisma and
dynamism that, like Plato, placed her above ordinary mortals.
In another letter, Synesius expresses how much he longs to
hear from her. He uses hyperbolic terms:

Your silence has been added to the sum of my sorrows. I
have lost my children, my friends, and the goodwill of
everyone. The greatest loss of all, however, is the
absence of your divine spirit. I had hoped that this
would always remain to me, to conquer both the
caprices of fortune and the evil turns of fate.

Or again, he is of the opinion that:

> Athens has no longer anything sublime except the country's famous names … Today Egypt has received and cherishes the fruitful wisdom of Hypatia. Athens was aforetime the dwelling-place of the wise; today the beekeepers alone bring it honor.

She could be tough too. There is a story that she deflated one student's heavy infatuation for her by rubbing his face in her menstrual blood. Whatever the truth of that, it is the case that her life was great because she lived in times that demanded great things of its key figures. She was to need all the courage and greatness she could muster. As her bloody story shows, there was a robust if not hard-hitting side to her character that could stand firm in the face of violence.

The background to what happened goes like this. A few years before her birth, Christianity had been declared the official religion of the empire. A period of uneasy pluralism was the result. The Egyptian triad of Serapis, Isis and Harpocrates were worshipped alongside the Christian Trinity of Father, Son and Holy Ghost.

Then, when she was in her thirties, civil war broke out in Alexandria, in part along religious lines. The city was not alone in suffering this violence. It was symptomatic of the historic shift that was underway, as the world finally moved from the Roman age and into the Christian. We can get some feeling for the times in another letter written by Synesius to Hypatia, in which he tells her of the tumult afflicting his city, also in North Africa, in modern-day Libya:

> I am encompassed by the sufferings of my city, and disgusted with her, for I daily see the enemy forces, and

men slaughtered like victims on an altar. I am breathing an air tainted by the decay of dead bodies. I am waiting to undergo myself the same lot that has befallen so many others, for how can one keep any hope, when the sky is obscured by the shadow of birds of prey?

In Alexandria, tensions reached a climax in about 390, when the bishop, Theophilus, issued a decree: no-one is to go to the pagan sanctuaries, or walk through the temples, it said. The bishop wished to seize these places of worship and make them churches, and his programme of reform led to bitter confrontations. There are tales of captivity, torture and killing on both sides. The Serapeum was apparently one of the major casualties of the conflict. Five hundred years old, it was the largest of the temples in the Greek quarter of the city, and housed an offshoot of the Mouseion. It represented a bastion for the old world, and whilst it stood, a bulwark against the new. It had to be razed, and it was. Christian power had scored a triumph, for to level the temples of a civilisation is to destroy its soul. However, it was but one battle in a longer war, and the Mouseion itself survived, at least for a while. It had endured several calamities in the past, and had already been completely rebuilt twice.

It was after the destruction of the Serapeum that Hypatia herself received the greatest honour of life. She was made head of the Platonic school in Alexandria. It was a poisoned chalice. Although the personal friend of Christian bishops, she was now firmly associated with the pagan side.

Things took another turn for the worse when Cyril, the nephew of Theophilus, became bishop in 412. An ambitious man who felt that holy ends justified the worst excesses of violent means, he needed a triumph to match that of his uncle Theophilus. He invested in a private army, veritable black-shirted 'shock troops': they were such a threat that the emperor himself demanded Cyril keep no more than 500, lest his own authority be challenged.

Cyril was opposed by Orestes, the Christian city prefect. Orestes represented secular imperial power that could also be ruthless, though it seems he tried to maintain some semblance of peace. But his powers were eroded. He was injured by a mob comprised of monks. (So paganism was not singled out for attack, and synagogues were ransacked too, as Jews were expelled from the city, their possessions stolen from them.)

Hypatia probably attempted to remain above the fray. For example, whilst not Christian, she did not object to the ecclesiastical seizing of temples. However, she was in a sense doubly suspect. It was not so much that she was a Hellenophile. Rather, it was a part of her expertise that proved problematic.

Her learning fell over several fields, on the one hand mathematics and astronomy, but on the other the mystical philosophy of Neoplatonism. Though Neoplatonism was incorporated into much Christian theology, especially in the Greek east, when combined with Egyptian occultism, as it was in Alexandria, it became an Hermetic system of thought that made some Christians very wary. Another bishop, John of Nikiu who lived somewhat later, saw only the work of the devil in her excellence. 'She was devoted at all times to magic, astrolabes and instruments of music, and she beguiled many people through Satanic wiles.' It is likely that Hypatia remained unmarried too, perhaps following Diotima to focus her energies on philosophy. But to many, her single status could be taken as more evidence of witchery.

Coupled to an association with Orestes, this proved to be a fatal combination. The rumour went about that she had counselled the prefect to fight the bishop. It was excuse enough for the thugs.

An account of what happened on that March day in 422 CE is given by Socrates Scholasticus:

> Some of them therefore, hurried away by a fierce and bigoted zeal, whose ringleader was a reader named Peter, waylaid her returning home, and dragging her from her carriage, they took her to the church called Caesareum, where they completely stripped her, and then murdered her with tiles. After tearing her body in pieces, they took her mangled limbs to a place called Cinaron, and there burnt them.

When the chronicler says they 'murdered her with tiles', he actually means they flayed her alive with oyster shells.

The killing came to be regarded as one of the worst acts in the history of early Christianity. Cyril himself was chastised for it. Contemporaries said that he was in danger of building a Satanic kingdom quite as revolting as the one he claimed to be casting aside, though it did not stop the Church making him a saint.

Voltaire felt moved to pray for Cyril: 'I beseech the merciful father to have pity on his soul.' Edward Gibbon, in his *Decline and Fall of the Roman Empire*, makes the episode totemic: 'The murder of Hypatia has imprinted an indelible stain on the character and religion of Cyril of Alexandria.' Cyril himself, Gibbon assumes, burned with jealousy at the brilliance of this wise woman, 'in the bloom of beauty, and in the maturity of wisdom'. For him, the story represented all that was best about the spiritual rationalism of the Greek world, coming to blows with all that is worst in the doctrinaire tendencies of barbaric Christianity.

Gibbon was wrong to see the world divided into two sides so neatly, but he is only the most famous of the Enlightenment men of letters to feel this way. The nineteenth-century French poet Leconte de Lisle was more explicit:

> The vile Galilean struck you and cursed you; But in falling, you became even greater! And now, alas! The spirit of Plato and the body of Aphrodite have withdrawn forever to the fair skies of Hellas!

Hypatia had become a pagan saint, martyred by Christianity. And yet alongside massively simplifying the picture of what happened, de Lisle's use of phrases such as 'the vile Galilean' themselves vent an undercurrent of violence. They perpetuate the same cycles of fear and hate, in literary form. Cyril himself might have envied their rhetorical power. One cannot help but feel that Hypatia, in whose honour they are supposedly written, would not. We can learn that first lesson on living in times of violence from her story.

After her death, intellectual life in Alexandria struggled for survival. The pagan world was clearly done for and the Christian proved to be a turbulent replacement, then at least. Sectarianism set in. Clerics squabbled; they despised and squandered their city's scholarly inheritance. History proved another truth about violence: it is not redemptive. It does not promote progress. There is no such thing as a benevolent revolution.

And then there is this: one of Hypatia's most noble sentiments in the face of violence is said to have been: 'Reserve your right to think, for even to think wrongly is better than not to think at all.' It is a worthy epitaph, to which we might insert an addendum: to be wronged for your thinking, even violently wronged, is better than not to think at all. Lesson three: keep thinking, keep philosophy alive.

CHAPTER 20

Socrates and being towards death

Dying by hemlock poisoning was one of the better ways to go, if you had to go at all. According to Xenophon it is 'the death which has been judged easiest or least painful'. Like having your pet put down, it was antiquity's equivalent of the kindly lethal injection. Unlike other methods of execution – beheading, crucifixion, stoning – it is bloodless. It is certainly better than Hypatia's fate of being flayed alive. By cutting out the need for gore, it is gentler on victim, family and friends. The individual could remain in command of his or her faculties, and importantly administer the cocktail themselves. Poise, reason and control were maintained to the last.

It offered the best exit for Socrates. He had been condemned and now was the day of his execution. Family and friends were comforted, or had been quietly escorted back home. Socrates was able to thank the jailer for his care. What should I do?, the philosopher asked, as the cup of poison was brought to him. 'You have only to walk about until your legs are heavy, and then lie down, and the poison will act,' the jailor replied. Thus, according to the moving account given in Plato's *Phaedo*:

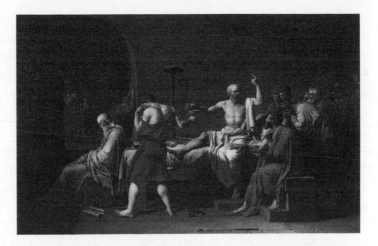

Figure 33 *The Death of Socrates* by Jacques-Louis David

he walked about until, as he said, his legs began to fail, and then he lay on his back, according to the directions, and the man who gave him the poison now and then looked at his feet and legs; and after a while he pressed his foot hard and asked him if he could feel; and he said, no; and then his leg, and so upwards and upwards, and showed us that he was cold and stiff. And he felt them himself, and said: When the poison reaches the heart, that will be the end. He was beginning to grow cold about the groin, when he uncovered his face, for he had covered himself up, and said (they were his last words) – he said: 'Crito, I owe a cock to Asclepius; will you remember to pay the debt?' 'The debt shall be paid,' said Crito; 'is there anything else?' There was no answer to this question; but in a minute or two a movement was heard, and the attendants uncovered him; his eyes were set, and Crito closed his eyes and mouth.

Thus, apparently, died the 'best of all the men'. 'I certainly found being there an astonishing experience,' reflects Phaedo. 'Although I was witnessing the death of one who was my friend, I had no feeling of pity, for the man appeared happy both in manner and words as he died nobly and without fear.' A rational death. A serene death. A good death. The sage was able to die as he had lived.

But just what did Socrates make of death, the one certainty that faces us all? What did he prescribe to prepare yourself for this inevitable event? In particular, did his contentment rest on an assurance of life everlasting?

An ancient Greek could draw on many different stories, and rehearse any number of metaphors, to talk about his or her passing. There was no one view, and even the same source might offer a variety of reflections – appropriate, really, given that no-one knows for sure what lies on the other side of the grave, if anything does at all.

Some were pessimistic. They described the afterlife as a ghostly experience, the immortal soul being a washed out version of mortal vitality. With sacrificial blood, poured out as libations by the living, it might regain some of its former energy. But mostly, this view held that life in the beyond is like a bat fluttering about in a grey cave, or a shadow creeping along a wall. The life-force gradually weakens as the shade fades out.

Others in antiquity were optimistic, at least for those who had lived well. The Elysian Fields were a glorious place in which the heroic dead could dwell happily. The climate was agreeable and life was easy. Homer, for one, versified the passage of mortals who were so blessed by the gods in the *Odyssey*. They were transported to the West, crossing the waters of Oceanus, passing the White Rock, before reaching a place of bliss at the Gates of the Sun, where they found meadows of green and lilac.

No surprise, then, that with the birth of philosophy came attempts to settle the matter. Should the death knell be feared or welcomed? Can more be discerned about what happens? These are the kind of questions philosophers asked. They are ones we ask still today. One thing to note is what was meant by the word 'soul'. It is initially best thought of as the same as 'mind', the incorporeal facet of the human individual, manifest, say, in language or thoughts or feelings or intentions. This does not necessarily imply a dualism between body and soul/mind. It might be just to say that there appear to be two aspects of the one united whole which is the human being: a tangible element that is embodied, and an intangible that is not. Neither does the word 'soul' necessarily imply immortality: the mind might well be mortal, dying with the body since it so stems from the body.

Pythagoreans provided one influential strand of speculation. This mystical tradition believed in life after death and further that death was but the route into another life. Followers of Pythagoras, including Plato, held to the transmigration of souls. In fact, the dying individual was about to embark upon a journey that would take three thousand years. His or her immortal soul, which in some sense carried the identity of the person, would move from creature to creature 'of land, sea and air', until it entered again into the body of another human being.

Pythagoras himself was said to have once passed by a puppy that was being whipped. He took pity upon it, calling out, 'Stop, do not beat it; for it is the soul of a dear friend – I recognized it when I heard its voice.' Another myth describes how he was first born as Euphorbus and then Hermotimus. As

Hermotimus, he decided to prove the reincarnation of the soul. He entered a temple and correctly identified the ancient owner of a shield, though the shield itself was thoroughly decayed. Hermotimus then became Pyrrhus, a fisherman, and then Pythagoras.

If you are inclined to an Eastern take on things, these tales can sound quite familiar. For example, enlightened individuals are said to have an ability to remember past lives. The belief in reincarnation linked in turn with Pythagorean vegetarianism. It fed into other metaphysical beliefs such as the notion of eternal recurrence, the doctrine that life is a succession of repeats, as evidenced by the perpetually returning sun or the run and rerun of the seasons.

Links between death, the soul and nature were made by philosophers in less esoteric ways too – a second strand – and these became important to the Stoics. Here, it was imagined that the human person is composed of an integrated body and soul too, though in this schema the soul was thought of as breaking down into what might now be called different functions of the mind – the emotive, the purposive, the conscious, the rational. This human microcosm is in turn a reflection of the macrocosm which is the universe itself. You could say that Stoics thought every human being contains a spark of life that shares in the life-force of the cosmos. They referred to it as *pneuma*, or breath and said that it spreads through an individual rather like the nervous system. As the human body is made of the same stuff as the physical world, so it followed that human beings share in the energy of the cosmos too. Humans are 'ensouled' as is the universe.

It's a theory a little like one that has emerged recently, called panpsychism. Panpsychism stems from the difficulty of explaining how the grey mush of the brain can give rise to the vivid experiences of the mind. The activity of neurons just seems entirely unlike the experience of being alive, for all that the two are deeply connected. So panpsychism postulates that matter and mind are actually two sides of the same coin, and that to some degree all matter can be said to be sentient, if not actually conscious. Our link with the rest of the universe is not just physical but mental.

The Stoics associated the density of matter with the physical heaviness of the body. The lightness of air, sky and space was associated with the intangible facets of the human mind or soul. Thus, it could leave the body at death and ascend into the heavens where, in a climactic synthesis, it would rejoin the totality of the cosmos. Preparing for death, then, was exactly the same thing as doing philosophy. Philosophy's aim was to live more and more according to reason, which they interpreted as aligning your own consciousness with that of the cosmic consciousness that pervades the universe, into which you might disperse when you die. The experience would be like a drop of wine dissipating in the ocean.

A third reflection took a different line again. The presocratic philosopher Democritus is the seminal figure here. His considered opinion was that absolute dissolution was the most likely thing to happen when we die. It is like the contemporary view that death is final and after it there is nothing at all.

The belief stems from his atomistic view of nature, that all things are made up of tiny, indivisible particles. Living matter, including human beings, is animated by a particular class of atom – 'soul atoms' – though they are subject to the same laws of disintegration as inert matter. At death, then, the body ceases to be able to maintain the intricate assemblage of atoms that is the definition of what it is to be alive. Soul atoms fly apart quite as surely as the flesh can be seen to disintegrate.

'Mortal nature dissolves,' was how Democritus summed up our fate. In fact, evidence that death leads to dissolution can be seen before death itself, for the disintegration of the body, which is the disintegration of its atoms, begins in old age. 'Old age is a general decrepitude,' he continued. So what to do? Be brave. Don't fear. Dissolution is natural. 'Men seem to reject the very thought of death because of a love of life – which derives from a terror of death, not from an enjoyment of life,' he reasoned.

The Epicureans, who followed the atomism of Democritus, popularised this approach. Not fearing death was one of their four principles for the happy life – along with not fearing gods, and realising that what you really need is easy to find, and that pain is generally easier to endure in actuality than it is in prospect.

Democritus is also a key figure in another quasi-scientific approach to the ultimate question. He is said to have examined the stories of 'those who are thought to have died and then come to life again'. Presumably he thought the evidence equivocal. However, others also developed this interest, in the sense of seeking testimonies of what might happen after we breathe our last from people who had apparently come back. They collected the accounts of people who had had near-death experiences. A handful survive and they make an arresting read.

Plato writes up a particularly dramatic one in the *Republic*. It concerns a brave man called Er the Pamphylian. He was a soldier and was left for dead in the field after a battle. The 'corpse' was not collected for ten days. When it was, it was noted that the body was still fresh. Nonetheless, two further days on, it was readied for the funeral pyre. However, Er was in a suspended state. Just before it was too late, he miraculously revived. The soul that had been separated from his body rejoined it. When it did, he spoke of things on the other side.

He remembered openings in the earth, meadows, rainbows and light, the toing and froing of the recently dead, stricken tears, happy greetings, judgement and the transmigration of souls. Er himself was told that he was to become a messenger and return to earth to tell of these things to his fellows. Plato relates the story, or myth, because it fits with an idea he had about what might happen after death. As he develops the testimony in the *Republic*, it is the possibility that the dead are judged which most interests him.

Another such tale is recorded by Plutarch. One Thespesius of Soli had apparently died as a result of a blow to the head. However, three days later, again at his funeral, he came round:

> He saw nothing like what he had seen before: the stars were enormously large, and immeasurably far from one another, and they shone forth with a light of great force and marvellous colours, so that the soul, gently and lightly transported by this light like a ship on a calm sea, could quickly move to wherever it wished.

Near death experiences were controversial then, and they still are now. One current experiment to test NDEs has hidden images close to the ceilings in hospital emergency rooms, the kind of place where they are likely to happen. When NDEs are reported, subjects will be asked whether they saw these images, and if so, what they were. It will be interesting to see what the scientists conclude, though I suspect that the experiments will settle nothing.

Perhaps reason can help, though. This is what the man who drank hemlock relied upon to shape his attitudes about all manner of things. So what did the historical Socrates conclude about death?

It is hard to say for sure. Scholars have typically argued that he must have believed in the immortality of the soul. He would have held that the soul inhabited the body as the life-force which animated it. Once the soul had departed, the body was as much meat – which would explain why Socrates told his followers not to perform any funeral rituals for him. The soul continues into the afterlife, and whether it will be amongst the blessed or the cursed of Tartarus only the gods can tell.

However, a closer examination of the texts in which Plato has Socrates discuss death suggests that these ideas were more Plato's and that Socrates was agnostic about human immortality. In the *Apology*, the Platonic dialogue that is probably the closest to the historical Socrates, he insists that he has no privileged knowledge about death. He mostly goes on what people say. And since some say life in eternity is better than this life, and others say it is a fate far worse, he must conclude that he doesn't know. Moreover, there are plenty of other things about which mortals can gain a better grasp, not least the immediate business of living well. In fact, in tackling them, death might become a lot easier to deal with too, as seems to have been the case with Socrates himself, for he is also quite clear that he doesn't fear it.

He wryly confirms this agnosticism when he asks the friends who came to visit him on his last day whether they or he are going to have the better day. They have to mourn his loss. He, though, is dying and that will at least be an adventure. So vivid is that moment of dark humour that it strikes me as a joke that Socrates actually made.

One can push a little further into Socrates' opinion. For if he is sure he knows nothing for sure, he can still express a hope as to our post-mortem status. And that hope appears to have veered just on the side of immortality. What he argues is this.

First, there is no reason to fear death, as some people do, as if it were the worst thing that could possibly befall you. This is because if no-one knows what happens when we die, then to fear death, is to fear what you can only guess at. '[But] people fear [death] as if they knew it were the greatest evil,' he says. A guess is never substantiated, and in the case of death, not open to substantiation. So the fear is equally ill-founded.

Second, if death is the end, then it will presumably be like a dreamless sleep. In life, spending the dark hours in dreamless rest is usually referred to as a 'good night's sleep'. Death, in this case, can therefore be called good too.

Third, if it turns out that death is not the end, then Socrates concludes it is something to look forward to. For one thing, he has dedicated his life to doing the best for his soul; that is what philosophy has been for him – shaking off delusion, deepening his self-knowledge, pursuing the good in life. In fact, his strong sense was that philosophy is a divinely sanctioned activity, since it is the best strategy for the pursuit of the good life for humankind. He believed that it is possible to taste, even embody, the good in this life, if you pursue the right way of life. So he can be confident that his soul is in the best shape it could possibly be for death. Further, if he lives on after death, then presumably he will find himself to be with others similar to himself, and with those others he will be able to continue as he has lived, namely in conversation, only now with great judges and poets and heroes. That, he says, would bring him 'inconceivable happiness'. Thus, whilst the other options are not bad, he hopes for what he regards as the best.

And yet: no mortal can ever know for sure. Hence his agnosticism.

But if the question cannot be definitively answered, there is value in embracing an ambivalent position and not feeling

Figure 34 Socrates with two students, thirteenth-century image

compelled to settle the matter one way or another. This leads to another strand in the ancient philosophers' reflections on death that was almost common to all, namely its significance for how you live your life now.

Death was of perennial interest to them not only because of the imperative to explore what might happen. As the ultimate fact about life, it is bound to be a key ingredient, even the determining element, in any practice of life they advanced. 'To philosophise is to learn how to die,' was the common formula. Marcus Aurelius had a slightly different emphasis: 'Let your every deed and word and thought be those of one who might depart from this life this very moment.'

It sounds bleak. But the practice was not supposed to induce depression. Quite the opposite. 'Let death be before your eyes every day, and you will never have any abject thought nor excessive desire,' advised Epictetus. Seneca drew out the positive too:

When we are about to go to sleep, let us say in joyful cheerfulness: 'I have lived; I have travelled the route that fortune had assigned to me.' If God should grant us tomorrow as well, let us accept it joyfully. That person is most happy and in tranquil possession of himself who awaits tomorrow without worries. Whoever says: 'I have lived', gets up every day to receive unexpected riches.

The contemplation of death is a liberation. It confronts a fear that lurks in every soul, and by staring it in the face, potentially undoes it. The unexpected thing that happens in the process is that it throws the emphasis back onto the gift of life. The early Christians picked up on that dynamic too. Saint Anthony told his disciples, 'Live as though you were dying every day.' He was not death-obsessed; rather he understood life.

One can see something of what this can mean from the accounts of people who have faced death and in the horror of that experience found sources of goodness they previously did not know. Fred Burnham, who came close to dying on 9/11, provides one such testimony. Trapped underground in a building near the twin towers, he was finding breathing increasingly difficult. He calculated he had about fifteen minutes of air left, and then began to realise that he would die.

He was with others, and suddenly they felt bonded together in love. It was then that he experienced death's freedom:

No fear. And I discovered for the first time that I am not afraid of death and that has totally changed my life. My experience, my every breath from that moment on has been different from anything prior to that. That transformative moment, discovering that you are not afraid to die, can ... totally transfigure your life.

This account comes in Rupert Shortt's biography of Rowan Williams, the Archbishop of Canterbury, *Rowan's Rule*: one of the people Fred Burnham was with was Dr Williams. The next day, the archbishop preached about the experience, and he analysed death's liberty in this way:

> It seems to me that when we are faced with the real, concrete possibility that death is going to happen to us, we immediately have one of the deepest possible challenges posed to the way … we think about ourselves. We're brought up against a situation in which we have no ability at all to think about the future.

To be confronted by death is to see the end coming towards you. Suddenly there is no future. That termination is to be forced to think radically differently about the value of life. The habit that most have is to live in the future, or for the future, or oppressed by the future. Taking a lead from Buddhism, Williams concludes that when the future goes, all that is left is compassion. It is as if a new moral space opens up and it can be filled with tranquillity, delight and empathy. All this is not to say that facing death is not a terrible experience, let alone to mitigate the true horrors of 9/11 and other catastrophes, great and small. Far from it. Death is real. There is nothing more real. And yet, it is because of its granite quality that it provides this tremendous opportunity to reframe life. That is perhaps the transfiguration felt by Fred Burnham. It is perhaps what the ancient philosophers sought in their choice to contemplate death.

There is a related element that mortality highlighted for the philosophers of antiquity – less existential, more intellectual. For most of them, death was closely associated with gaining a cosmic vision of things, of being able to conceive of the universe in its totality. This perspective is valuable since it is to gain a proper perspective on yourself and your life, notably in its smallness. Such a flight of the imagination is desirable and illuminating regardless of what you think of death itself. Lucretius the Epicurean, who believed that death was nothing at all, still sought eternal contemplation:

Since space stretches far beyond the boundaries of the world, into the infinite, our mind seeks to sound out what lies within this infinity, in which the mind can plunge its gaze at will, and to which the mind's thoughts can soar in free flight.

This vantage point is brought to life in a story by Lucian, called *Icaromenippus*, featuring the humourous Cynic, Menippus. In it, he realises that the problem with much philosophy is that it is pursued by people whose feet are too firmly on the ground. Hence, for all that they claim for themselves, they are in fact:

no sharper-sighted than their neighbors, some of them purblind, indeed, with age or indolence; and yet they say they can distinguish the limits of the sky, they measure the sun's circumference, take their walks in the supra-lunar regions, and specify the sizes and shapes of the stars as though they had fallen from them.

Menippus decides he needs wings, and so builds himself some. He conducts some test flights and after a few reaches so high that he gets to the moon. He looks back to earth and sees how insignificant are the preoccupations of most men and women. He has gained a cosmic, more objective view of things:

You must often have seen a community of ants, some of them a seething mass, some going abroad, others

> coming back to town. One is a scavenger, another a
> bustling porter loaded with a bit of bean-pod or half a
> wheat grain. They no doubt have, on their small ant-like
> scale, their architects and politicians, their magistrates
> and composers and philosophers. At any rate, what men
> and cities suggested to me was just so many ant-hills.

This sentiment is one consolation of philosophy. It is related to the consolation of science too, the liberty that comes from learning that in one sense you are actually nothing much at all; of realising that aeons existed before you, and will do afterwards. It is the opposite of the self-centred life of the individualist, and the burgeoning anxieties of the solipsist, for whom meaning can only come from one place, when that place – themselves – is, on the whole, such a mean place.

So how did the ancient philosophers, and Socrates in particular, recommend that we pursue this contemplation of our being towards death, to borrow Heidegger's phrase? What practices did they teach to coax one to embracing its bittersweet reality?

A first might be to treat death as if it were, in fact, real. That might sound an odd thing to suggest, especially to those who are facing death in some way. However, there is a perverse feature of death that makes this practice important: in life, you cannot experience your own death. You may have intimations of it, not least in the tragic death of others – though psychologists will tell you that part of the agony of mourning is the uncomfortable realisation that you will live on. That is why surviving such losses takes courage. Wittgenstein famously put it this way: 'Death is not an event in life. It is not experienced.' But deliberately treating death as real is a way of negotiating this *impasse*.

Doing so in small ways is advisable. The ancients found opportunities in surprising places. Take logic. Aristotle is well known for his analysis of logic, indeed for being the first to assemble a system of logic. Logic might seem like a dry subject, far from the vicissitudes of human life. And yet, Aristotle's famous syllogism – how two premises can lead to a valid conclusion – has forever become linked to a practice of death. I do not know who first gave this example, but it is the standard: 'All humans are mortal. Socrates is human. Therefore Socrates is mortal.' In a small way, it reminds us of death in life.

A second exercise is a little more confrontational, one for those who have become somewhat accustomed to the prospect of death. It is to contemplate life as if close to death, and thereby attempt to look it in the eye, in your mind's eye. Two benefits follow from this that we have touched on already. First, it highlights the present. Second, death itself comes to seem less daunting.

The fundamental reason why this sensibility can emerge is because to contemplate being on the verge of death is to realise the truth of your own finitude, your own mortality. It is the truth that sets you free. Even if you believe in some kind of life after death, the fundamental truth still obtains, that to be human is to be a being towards death. What you make of death itself, regardless of what might come after, is a key question of life. Even if you reach a point at which you make nothing of it at all, you must still go through the process. To *simply* make nothing of it at all, by denial or complacency, is not to deal with death. Paradoxically, it is to live as if you are immortal even when you don't intellectually believe in immortality.

The ancient philosophers came to different conclusions as a result of this practice. Marcus Aurelius could on occasion stare death in the face and in it he discerned a natural process. Being a Stoic, he regarded this as good: for him, acknowledging the inevitability of death is not to be fatalistic, it is to align yourself with processes you can trust:

> Consider what it is to die; and that, if one looks at death in and of itself, dissolving the images associated with death by taking apart our common conception of it, he will not suspect it to be anything other than a product of nature.

Cicero did something similar, though it precipitated a different thought. His reflections led him to discern the vanity of a life that attempts to trump death in worldly achievements. Ironically enough, this was something he knew about. He spent much of his life trying to succeed at the power-politics of the late Roman Republic, and since we are still reading his words today, you might argue the strategy worked, at least to a degree. However, his point was not that life should be without achievements. It is a question of what achievements you choose. The right choice, he felt, is only made when coupled to an existential awareness of death. This was the consciousness he developed when he realised the game was up for him in Rome. He left for his house in the country, in effect to wait for his death, and then produced most of his best philosophy:

> This is the worst of their torments – they find that they have longed in vain for money, power, and glory; for they have not derived any pleasure from these things, which they hoped for so passionately and worked so hard to attain.

A third exercise is the most subtle way of practising death. It is the one that it's possible Socrates made his own, and can be stated simply. He took death to be what he hoped for, if he didn't know for sure, namely the separation of the soul from the body. And the exercise that followed was to practise that separation as if it were true and see where the exploration led. How might that be done? In a word, meditation.

It's possible that such a practice was first championed by the presocratic philosopher Parmenides. It's a controversial claim, but according to the scholar Peter Kingsley, Parmenides was an *iatromantis*, a healer-prophet, who practised the art of incubation, that is physical and mental stillness in order to be initiated into the undivided stillness of all reality. In ancient hospitals, which were also temples to the god Asclepius, people who were ill might be cured by being induced into a deep sleep. Parmenides seems to have believed that this practice was not just useful as a remedy for diseases, but for life and death itself.

According to Kingsley, Parmenides developed incubation techniques so that they became a kind of 'death before death'. His only surviving text is a poem in which he describes the resulting experience. It recounts a journey to the abode of a goddess. Led by the daughters of Helios, and pulled on a chariot with a team of mares, he traverses 'the far-fabled path of the divinity' to the halls of Night. Parmenides continues:

> And the goddess received me kindly, and in her hand she took my right hand, and she spoke and addressed me thus: 'O young man, accompanied by immortal charioteers and mares who bear you as you arrive at our abode, welcome, since a fate by no means ill sent you ahead to travel this way.'

Miraculously, or at least imaginatively, he travelled to the judgement seat, the place where immortals dwell and the souls of the dead are sent. He 'survived' the separation of soul from body and 'returned' to tell of it.

Of course, it is impossible to know what to make of this mysterious trip. It is related in a language that is almost entirely opaque to us today. Luckily, though, Plato leaves an account of a related and more comprehensible practice. Moreover, he says it was the one favoured by Socrates.

It seems that being towards death was embraced by Socrates no more keenly than through meditation. In several passages in different dialogues, Plato describes what the exercise was like. Here's one from the *Phaedo*:

> [It] consists in separating the soul as much as possible from the body, and accustoming it to withdraw from all contact with the body and concentrate itself by itself, and to have its dwelling, so far as it can, both now and in the future, along by itself, freed from the shackles of the body.

Now, that might be thought as clear as mud. However, Socrates seems to have had an ability to see beyond or through the experience of being embodied, all the while remaining embodied, of course. In that sense it was an imaginative separation of the soul. Another quotation develops the thought:

> The soul can best reflect when it is free of all distractions such as hearing or sight or pain or pleasure of any kind – that is, when it ignores the body and becomes as far as possible independent, avoiding all physical contacts and associations as much as it can, in its search for reality … The body intrudes … into our investigations, interrupting, disturbing, distracting, and preventing us from getting a glimpse of the truth.

The key issue here is the handling of the 'body's intrusion'. It might be thought that the aim is to be free of all distractions, which is to say that the practice was some kind of denial of the body. This is what many scholars today do in fact conclude. However, whilst Socrates is undoubtedly stepping out of himself in some way – allowing the mind to soar in free flight, as Lucretius put it, seeking that cosmic view – the way he might have achieved that state is actually by paying attention to the body. It is only when you are aware of the interruptions, disturbances and distractions of the body that you can set them to one side, not because they cease but because you have become fully conscious of them. If you try simply to ignore them, they dominate. In other words, the first step in this practice is to turn to the body; to make it the primary object of contemplation. Then, as the body is explored, the result is that a different experience can come through.

The way to contemplate the body is by keeping still. This would be a link with Parmenides. Again, that is not a way of denying the body but of precisely drawing attention to it. If you have never tried it, do. Even a few minutes held in a still pose will alert you to all sorts of twinges, gurgles and aches that are usually mostly hidden.

There are a number of accounts that survive of Socrates apparently doing this very thing. Moreover, he was good at it, remaining transfixed for hours, not just minutes. Here's one recorded by Aulus Gellius in *Attic Nights*. The description is based upon another given by Plato in the *Symposium*:

> Among voluntary tasks and exercises for strengthening his body for any chance demands upon its endurance we are told that Socrates habitually practised this one: he would stand, so the story goes, in one fixed position, all day and all night, from early dawn until the next sunrise, open-eyed, motionless, in his very tracks and with face

and eyes riveted to the same spot in deep meditation, as
if his mind and soul had been, as it were, withdrawn
from his body.

It is easy, I think, to misunderstand these exercises in motion-
lessness – given that this interpretation is right. For example,
Xenophon made what I suspect is the mistake of confusing an
essentially spiritual exercise with one of sheer fortitude. To
him, Socrates was:

the most self-controlled of men in respect of his sexual
and other appetites; then he was most tolerant of cold
and heat and hardships of all kinds; and finally he had so
trained himself to be moderate in his requirements that
he was very easily satisfied with very slight possessions.

What Xenophon apparently fails to see is that this self-
control is not admirable for its own sake. It is as a preparation
for death that it makes sense.

Similarly, it would be wrong to view Socrates as an ascetic.
Plato attempts to reduce the risk of that in the way he portrays
Socrates. For example, in the *Symposium*, the story of the drinking party, Socrates imbibes alcohol along with the rest of the
guests. Moreover, they remark at how well Socrates holds his
drink. By the end of the evening – which had become the next
morning – Socrates is the only one not to have fallen asleep. He
leaves at dawn, the dialogue concludes, to embrace the new day
in the way that he always did, apparently no worse for wear.

The point is that the Socratic sage will enjoy bodily pleasures.
The aim is not to reject anything. It is to see through them. In no
context does this become clearer than in the perception of how
being human is being towards death.

Meditation continued to be practised in successive genera-
tions at Plato's Academy. Diogenes Laertius tells us that
Xenocrates, Plato's successor, 'would retire into himself more
than once a day and would devote, it is said, a whole hour to
silence.' The practice left him 'singularly free from pride,'
Diogenes remarks. Xenocrates' successor, Polemo, had a similar habit.

So it turns out that Socrates' message on death is straightforward, and penetrating in that simplicity. Whatever you make
of it, whatever your view of life after death, however you feel
that tight association called body and soul ends up – rotting in
the earth or rising to the heavens – this question is a constant:
how, in this life, are you to grip the reality of death? Choose a
practice. He recommended philosophy as a way of life. But do
practise one. Why? Because the contemplation of death leads to
life, here and now. Who knows about the hereafter?

Index